I Come to Teach!

A Comprehensive Guide and Planner for Substitute Teachers and Program Coordinators

Geneva G. Cannon

First Edition

Avenegg, Inc.
Salisbury, Maryland

I Come to Teach!
A Comprehensive Guide and Planner for Substitute Teachers and Program Coordinators
Geneva Cannon

Published by:
Avenegg, Inc.
1147 S. Salisbury Blvd., Ste. 8
PMB 142
Salisbury, MD 21801 USA
Orders@aveneggincpublishing.com
http://www.aveneggincpublishing.com

© 2006 by Geneva Cannon
Printed in the United States of America
Library of Congress Number: 2006905989
ISBN 0-9785091-0-2

Cover Design by Alpha Advertising - Tel: 1-217-288-9477
Author's photograph by Gary Marine Photography - Tel: 1-410-546-5551

Publisher's Cataloging-in-Publication Data
(Provided by Quality Books, Inc.)

Cannon, Geneva.
  I come to teach! : a comprehensive guide and planner
    for substitute teachers and program coordinators /
  Geneva G. Cannon. — 1st ed.
  p. cm.
  Includes index.
  LCCN 2006905989
  ISBN 0-9785091-0-2

  1. Substitute teachers—United States—Handbooks, manuals, etc.   I. Title.
  LB2844.1.S8C36 2006   371.14'122
  QBI06-600277

Attention: Corporations, Nonprofit Organizations, and Schools

I Come to Teach! is available at quantity discount with bulk purchase for educational, business, nonprofit, or sales promotional use. For information, please contact Avenegg, Inc. At the time of contact, please provide the title of the book, the ISBN, the quantity of books that you are ordering, how the book will be used and by whom, and the date needed.

Dedication

Education is not the filling of a pail, but the lighting of a fire.
-William Butler Yeats (1865-1939)

With respect and gratitude, I dedicate this book to all the enthusiastic teachers and substitute teachers who inspire, motivate, and educate our children in today's classrooms.

About the Author

Geneva Cannon

Geneva is an educator, with years of experience as a classroom teacher, a staff development coordinator, a secondary instructional supervisor, and a trainer of substitute teachers. Currently, she is the President of Avenegg, Inc., an educational publishing and consulting firm in Salisbury, Maryland, that specializes in the training of substitute teachers.

In 1984, Geneva authored her first publication, *A Survival Guide for Substitute Teachers*. This work emphasized the importance of substitute teachers in education. Later, she authored *How to Survive Your Substitute Teaching Experience*, a practical guide filled with tips and strategies for beginning and experienced substitute teachers.

Most recently, Geneva published *Caring for Your Loved One Who Is Ill at Home,* a 268-page guide and planner for family caregivers and personal home care assistants. This book details the decisions, challenges, and opportunities that she faced during the eight years she and others cared for her mother, who passed away recently as a result of Alzheimer's disease and the accompanying related complications.

Geneva's passion for her work is best seen and felt in her training workshops. She is energizing and inspiring. Whether she is conducting a workshop for substitute teachers or a session for persons who are in the throes of caring for a loved one who is ill at home, her participants leave motivated and encouraged to integrate into their experiences the practical, ready-to-use information they receive.

Contents

Introduction

Who is teaching in today's schools when full-time teachers are away from their classrooms for personal and professional reasons? You and other substitute teachers like you are filling many of these positions.

To ensure your success and the success of your counterparts with students, numerous school districts are providing materials, in-service workshops, and continuing professional development training activities to enhance your performance in the classroom. As a result, you are learning how to manage classrooms more effectively. You are becoming more skilled in the use of teaching strategies and techniques. You are becoming more adept at teaching the full-time teacher's lesson plans, and you are learning how to creatively develop and successfully implement filler-activities, when lesson plans are unavailable.

I wrote ***I Come to Teach!*** to support what school districts are doing to help you plan and organize your teaching experiences, and enhance the *quality* of your performance in the classroom. I also wrote ***I Come to Teach!*** to support, especially, the beginning and veteran substitutes who are *excited* about substitute teaching and are searching for better ways to "thrive" in today's classrooms.

To this end, I have based this book on the following beliefs about substitute teachers:

1. You are vital educational assistants in today's schools. You are not educational student-sitters.
2. You are integral in the education of all children.
3. You will give your best in a learning environment if you, first and foremost, understand your roles as substitute teachers, and then, if school districts give you the professional training, materials, and support that you need to succeed.
4. Who you are in classrooms as *human beings* is often more important to students than what you know about the subject matter.
5. You understand that thorough preparation for the classroom experience is critical to effective substitute teaching and student learning.

I hope ***I Come to Teach!*** gives you new insights and confirms others. Let me hear from you. I would like to know how well the materials are working for you and how Avenegg, Inc., can further support all you do for students. Please contact us.

Disclaimer

I Come to Teach! is provided by Avenegg, Inc., for information purposes only and is intended to be used solely as a guide and planner for substitute teachers in a classroom setting, and for those individuals and groups that assist them.

There is an enormous amount of information in print and in other media on substitute teaching. You are encouraged to research and study what is available. Learn from the information. Ask questions and seek answers.

As you read and use the information in this presentation, please remember the following:

1. Avenegg, Inc. and its representatives do not provide professional advice, for which you, as substitute teachers, and those who work with you should seek professional services.

2. The author does not attempt, in the writing of this book, to address all of the issues and concerns regarding substitute teachers and teaching. Every substitute teaching experience is different. You are strongly encouraged to consult with the school principal and other appropriate administrators, and professionals in the districts that you serve, whenever you need assistance.

3. The ideas and materials provided in this presentation are not foolproof. There are no guarantees, expressed or implied, that the information contained in this book is appropriate for your substitute teaching experiences.

4. Schools have certain policies and procedures they are required to follow. It is important that you understand those policies and procedures, and the extent that the information in this book is compatible and supportive.

We have made every attempt in the writing, editing, and publishing of *I Come to Teach!* to provide you with accurate and timely information. Please understand that errors and omissions occur in printed materials. Therefore, errors and omissions may occur in this book.

The author of *I Come to Teach*! and the publisher, Avenegg, Inc., and its representatives shall assume no liability for any loss or alleged loss, or damage caused, or alleged damage caused to any person or group, directly or indirectly, by the information in this book. If you do not wish to accept these terms, you may return the book, unmarked and undamaged, to the publisher within 15 days from the shipping date, along with your sales slip, for a full refund of the purchase price. Before returning the item, please call 1-410-572-8801 for further instructions on returning books.

Chapter 1

How to Acquire a Substitute Teaching Position

*One hundred years from now, it will not matter what my
bank account was, how big my house was, or what kind of
car I drove. But the world may be a little better, because
I was important in the life of a child.*
-Forest Witcraft (1894-1967)

School districts are interested in hiring only the *best-qualified* people available to fill substitute teaching positions. How, then, can you prove to the school system where you want to teach that you are one of the *best*? Here are a few tips to help you get started:

How and Where to Begin: Before You Apply for a Position

Convey a Professional Attitude about Substitute Teaching

When you actively seek an available position in a school district, communicate your thoughts about the profession, with conviction, to teachers, principals, and interviewers. Say to everyone during your conversations such things as

- I *want* to teach.
- I know that I can make a positive difference in the lives of young people.
- I enjoy working with diverse groups of students.
- I believe all children can learn if schools give them the time, material, and support they need.
- I want to participate in rigorous and challenging professional development programs that will help me improve my substitute teaching skills.

I Come to Teach!

Become Familiar with the School and the District You Want to Serve

It is important that you become familiar with the school district, and more particularly, the schools you want to serve in the system before you apply for a substitute teaching position.

- Attend the district's board of education meetings, parent meetings, co-curricular activities, and public forums regarding various educational issues.
- Read everything available to you about the school and the district. Read annual reports, brochures, and other published materials.
- Visit the school's website, the district's website, and the state department of education's website to gather information.
- Volunteer to serve on school advisory committees and in booster clubs.
- Talk to principals, teachers, and other school personnel, including current substitute teachers.
- Talk to parents and other people in the community.
- Visit the school during open house or American Education Week.

Learn as much as you can to become informed and stay informed.

Learn What the Educational Prerequisites Are to Substitute Teach in the School District, Before You Apply for a Position

What will the district require of you before you can substitute teach in the system? Determine, for example, if the district will require you to:

- Have a teacher's license or certificate
- Become state-certified as a substitute teacher
- Complete certain courses or earn a specific number of college credits
- Have a degree from an accredited college or university
- Complete district-level substitute teacher training

To learn what the prerequisites are in a school district for persons who are interested in becoming substitute teachers in the system, call the district office to speak to a staff person in the Human Resources Department who has responsibility for the substitute teacher program. You may also visit the district's website for information. Make every attempt to *speak* with someone about the prerequisites, because, during the conversation, the person will probably give you additional ideas that you will not necessarily receive from the district's website.

Hone Your Skills

It is also important that you enhance your personal and professional skills, if necessary, before you apply for a substitute teaching position. Take a workshop or enroll in a course or two at your local college or university. Not only will the information look great on your resume, but it will also convey to school administrators that (a) you take the substitute teaching profession seriously, and (b) you want to perform well in the classroom.

How to Apply for a Substitute Teaching Position

Call the district office for information, or log on to the school district's website to learn what tasks you will need to complete to apply for a substitute teaching position. You may be required to do the following things:

- Complete an application
- Submit a resume
- Interview for a position
- Undergo a criminal background check
- Complete withholding and employment forms
- Provide one or more photo identifications (e.g., passport, driver's license)
- Provide corroborating documentation (e.g., birth certificate, social security card)
- Provide educational documentation (e.g., teaching certificate)
- Undergo health screenings (e.g., tuberculosis examination or other medical tests)

Obtain and Complete the Job Application

Usually, school districts provide several ways for interested persons to obtain applications for substitute teaching positions. Some systems provide applications at the district office. To obtain a copy, an individual can call the Human Resources Department at the district office and ask to have an application mailed to his or her address. The person may also be able to obtain an application by visiting the office. Many districts are placing printable copies on their websites, so that an individual can download and print the form, within seconds, from his or her computer.

After you obtain the application and other materials that you need to complete and return to the school district:

- **Duplicate the job application and other forms**. Put away the original materials, and use your duplicates as working drafts.
- **Read all materials carefully**. Give special attention to any open-ended questions on the application. These questions may require you to write a short paragraph in response. Make sure you understand the questions before you begin to write your answers. Highlight questions that have multiple parts, as a reminder to answer each part.
- After you read the application and all of the supporting forms carefully, **fill out your duplicate copies (working drafts)**. On these drafts, make all the mistakes and changes you want. You can strikeover words, draw arrows, doodle, write notes in the margins,

and more. You can do whatever you desire on your working drafts as long as you get your thoughts on paper.

- **Proofread your working draft carefully.** This can be a very tedious task because it is difficult at times to actually see your own mistakes. I suggest that you put away your working draft for an hour or more. Then, look at your work again. What is your initial reaction after you reread the draft? Are you pleased with what you have written? If you are not satisfied, make additional revisions and then lay the draft aside again for another hour or more. If you review your draft for the third time and find that you are still not pleased, ask a close friend who is skilled in proofreading to read your draft and provide you with constructive feedback. Then, you can work together on the final copy.
- **Complete the original copy of your application and other forms.** An application produced on a typewriter or a computer is the easiest to read and change as necessary. Consider hand printing your application. Write clearly and neatly. Keep your application and other forms free of stains and smudges. When you have completed all forms, make and keep copies of everything for your file. Then **place all materials that you plan to return neatly in a presentation folder. Place the folder in a 9 x 12 envelope. Make your materials aesthetically pleasing.** The completed application and materials are a reflection of you. Those items represent you. How well your materials are prepared and packaged will tell the receiver and the reviewer a great deal about you, especially about your thoroughness, your accurateness, and your organizational skills. So, take a little extra time to make a powerful first impression.
- **Return your completed application and all other forms <u>before the specified deadline</u>.** If you mail your materials, send everything by certified, priority mail. The receiver of your package will be required to sign for it. The U. S. Postal Service will return the signed certification slip to you. That slip is your receipt and verifies that a specific person at the district office received your material.

If you are required to fax your materials to a specific person at the district office, attach a cover page addressed to the individual. Ask the person to reply, confirming the receipt of your information.

Consider returning your application in person, Take every opportunity to let people in the office, who are involved in the hiring process (including secretaries and receptionists), know that you are interested in becoming a substitute teacher in the district. Let them sense your enthusiasm and passion.

Prepare the Resume

The resume that you develop will be a snapshot of your qualifications. The primary purpose for having this marketing tool is to help you obtain an interview. How well you prepare your resume will greatly determine whether you will receive an interview. So, give careful consideration and energy to this task. Here are a few tips and strategies worth remembering:

- Keep your resume brief and concise.
- Keep the format of your resume appealing and easy to read.
- List your work history experiences and your community service activities with the most recent first. Then, elaborate by including dates, positions, and responsibilities.
- Write your resume to mirror as closely as possible the specific requirements of the substitute teaching position for which you are applying.
- Include the names, addresses, and telephone numbers of three references in your resume. Use only the names of individuals who have given you their permission. Your references should be people who know you well and can write about your work habits, your skills, your community service, and your character. These individuals can be current or former coworkers, former employers, or community leaders. Do not use family members and friends as references.
- Print (computer-generate or photocopy) your resume onto quality bond paper; use the same quality of paper for your application letter.

Prepare the Application Letter

The application letter that you develop will serve as the cover letter for your resume. Its primary use is to provide the reviewer with an introduction to your resume which, we hope, will open the door for an interview.

Your letter should be brief, about one computer-generated page. Write your letter in a business letter format, and print the final draft on the same kind of quality bond paper that you used for your resume. Include the following information in your letter:

1. The position for which you are applying
2. A synopsis of your qualifications
3. Your availability for an interview

Before you begin developing your resume and application letter, visit your public library or a local bookstore to study various samples. Also, browse through the templates of sample resumes and application letters on your computer.

Prepare the Portfolio

The portfolio is the single most important marketing tool that you can develop and use in your interview to increase your chances of obtaining a substitute teaching position. The resume that you have developed is a snapshot of you. The portfolio that you develop will be an enlarged and expanded snapshot of you. This marketing tool includes detailed information about your experiences and achievements as well as any special work-related and community service recognitions that you have received.

Your portfolio should be neatly prepared and placed in a quality, 8½ x 11, three-ring binder. Keyboard the narrative information in your portfolio, and print all the material on quality bond paper. Photocopy any certificates and citations. Do not include original documents or confidential information. Insert your pages into protector sheets. Keep your portfolio to approximately twenty pages. Keep it brief. Let your portfolio speak for you.

You may wish to include the items on the following page in your portfolio.

I Come to Teach!

Contents of the Portfolio

Introduction

Include in this section
- a cover letter introducing your portfolio
- a table of contents
- your philosophy of education

Resume

- Include a copy of the same resume that you submitted with your application letter.

Educational Background

- Include a photocopy of your high school diploma or your college degree and any certifications that you have received in the profession or in related areas.

Experiences

- Write a *brief* overview of the experiences that you have had as a substitute teacher or in related areas during the past five to eight years.
- List the employment opportunities that you have had during the last eight years. Give the job title and the date you began and ended employment. Describe your major responsibilities. Begin with your most recent employment.
- List the community service activities that you have been involved in during the last eight years. Describe each activity, your role, and the duties you performed.

Sample Activities or Projects

- Include sample copies of substitute teaching projects or related projects that you have developed or have helped to develop. For example, you may wish to include filler-activities that you have developed or taught. Include photographs of special events or activities that show you teaching or working with children.
- Include sample projects and photographs from other related work or school experiences, if you have not worked in a classroom. Always obtain written permission from the appropriate sources before using the photographs in your portfolio.

Recognitions

- Include photocopies or cumulative lists of major certificates, citations, or other special recognitions.

Letters of Recommendation

- Include letters of recommendation from three people who know you well and who are willing to write specific things about your work habits, your skills, your community service, and your character traits. Do not use letters from friends or relatives.

Prepare for the Job Interview

Preparing for an interview for a substitute teaching position involves more than knowing the date, time, and location of the interview. Here are a few tips to consider:

1. **Learn as much as possible about the school district and the school that you want to serve before the interview.** Your interviewer will probably be impressed because you took the initiative to do a little extra research.

2. **Your portfolio can be an invaluable tool in an interview session. Practice using your portfolio before your interview.** Ask a family member or friend to help you rehearse. In some interviews, the interviewer sits across from the interviewee, at the table or desk. Have the person who is working with you sit across from you at a table or desk. Turn your portfolio so the pages are facing the person. The pages in the binder will be upside down to you. Now, practice scanning the material in your portfolio in this inverted order. Practice turning the pages of your binder. Your overall goal is to be as comfortable and as polished as possible when presenting your portfolio.

   If no one is available to help you practice, use an empty chair instead. Here is how you can use this technique: Place an empty chair at a table and then sit on the opposite side. Pretend the chair is the interviewer. Turn your portfolio toward the empty chair and begin practicing. Record or videotape your practice session and play it back when you finish rehearsing. Look or listen for those things that you did well on the practice tape and for those things that you need to improve.

As you practice, remember that a team of individuals may interview you. **How, then, do you use your portfolio with several people seated around the table?** When the interview begins, you will be able to identify the lead interviewer. If this person is sitting next to you or across from you, turn your portfolio toward this individual and begin. If the lead interviewer is sitting away from you, turn your portfolio to the person who is nearest you. As you speak, maintain good eye contact with everyone. Speak to the entire group regarding the contents of your portfolio. When you finish your presentation, circulate your portfolio to the other members of the group.

The interviewers may ask you to leave your portfolio so they can review your material later, especially if you have included photographs or tapes. At this point, determine how and when the interviewers will return the portfolio to you. If possible, return to the interview site for it.

Consider using multimedia to present your portfolio if you feel comfortable with, and proficient in, using the necessary technology. Discuss your intent to give this type of presentation at the time you schedule your interview. Also, schedule a time to set up the equipment at least 45 minutes prior to your interview. Use only equipment that you are thoroughly familiar with – preferably the equipment that you used during your practice sessions. Use only equipment that is in excellent operating condition. Make sure to take all accessories with you, including extension cords, power cords, and projection lamps.

You may have a chance to use your portfolio near the beginning of your interview. When the interviewer asks you, "Why do you feel qualified for the substitute teaching position?" Reply by saying, "Let me answer your question by *showing* you why I feel especially qualified for the position." Then, open your portfolio or turn on your multimedia presentation and begin.

3. **Try to anticipate the kinds of questions the interviewer is likely to ask.** In many interviews, the interviewer will begin by asking a relatively easy question to help you relax. Then the person will ask you the more difficult questions. These questions have multiple parts or are situational problems. Here are five sample questions that show this progression:

   - Why do you want to work as a substitute teacher in this school district?

- You have not substituted before; why do you believe you can be successful in this position?
- If you should be a successful candidate for one of the positions that we have available, what grade level, subject area, and academic level would you prefer to substitute teach?
- You have formed five cooperative learning teams in your class. Each team is composed of four students. You have given each team ten minutes to complete a task. After three minutes into the activity, four teams are working diligently. The other team has yet to begin. These students are engaged in an off-topic discussion. What do you do to redirect the students' attention to the assigned task?
- You are on the school playground with a pre-kindergarten class when a man walks up to you. He tells you that he is the father of one of the children on the playground and that he has come to take the child home, because her mother is ill. How do you think you will respond?

Use the above questions to practice. Ask a family member or friend who is a teacher or a school administrator to listen to your answers and give you constructive feedback. It is highly likely that you will not have these exact questions during your actual interview, but you will have similar questions that will test your ability to reason and make sound decisions.

When you practice answering the questions,

- Give **concise, on-topic answers.** Do not ramble or go on *ad nauseam*.
- **Ask the interviewer to repeat a question and to elaborate on it** if you do not understand what he or she has asked.
- **Maintain good eye contact** with the interviewers.

4. Before your interview, practice those things we often overlook and consider unimportant. These include:

- **How to enter the interview room:** Walk into the interview room with confidence. Stand tall and straight. Keep your shoulders back. Look confident. Carry your materials in an attaché. Wait until the interviewer asks you to sit. Then, sit down where the interviewer directs you.
- **How to open the interview:** The lead interviewer may introduce you to individual members of the interview team. Greet each interviewer with a warm "Hello," a friendly smile,

and a firm handshake. Again, maintain good eye contact with the person that you are greeting. If the lead interviewer introduces you to everyone collectively, greet the group with a warm "hello" and a friendly smile. Look at individual interviewers as you greet the group.

- **How to remain poised during the interview:** It is important that you look relaxed and professional when you enter the interview room, and maintain that posture throughout the interview. It is especially important for **you to pay careful attention to your body language.** Maintain an open posture that says, "I'm listening to you, and I am receptive to what you are saying." Do not fold your arms, even if the temperature in the room is below freezing. By folding your arms, you could convey to others that you are inflexible and set in your ways.

   Pay careful attention to your hands during the interview. Keep your hands still unless you are gesturing to make a point, taking notes, or doing something else that adds to the interview process. Do not tap your fingers on the table or twiddle your thumbs, play with a pen or a piece of clothing. These things indicate that you are nervous.

   An interviewer may ask you a very difficult question that you may need a few seconds to think about before you answer. If you should need a few extra seconds to formulate your answer, ask for that time. Please note that I said a "few" extra seconds, not minutes. Ask the interviewer to repeat the question and to clarify, if necessary. Make a note of each part of the question that you need to answer. Take a few seconds to think about what you will say. Organize your thoughts. Then take a deep breath and give your best answer.

- **How to end an interview:** Close the interview with "Thank you for this opportunity to interview." Maintain eye contact with the interviewers as you speak. After the interview, exit the room as you entered it – professionally and confidently. Do not stay longer to talk more about an interview question or about personal matters.

5. **Dress professionally on the day of the interview.** First impressions really count and often remain in an interviewer's mind long after the interview has ended. Choose the clothes and accessories that you will wear on the day of your interview well in advance. Your goal is to look better than your best, without looking overdressed. Dress in business blue or other appropriate business colors that make you look great. Above all, be neat and clean from head to toe.

6. **Know the time, date, and precise location of the interview.** Plan to arrive at the interview site at least 15 minutes before the scheduled time for the interview. If you plan to visit the restroom or get a drink of water before the interview begins, arrive even earlier.

7. **Get plenty of rest the night before the interview.** You know the number of hours of sleep your body requires. It is important that you remain alert in the interview from start to finish, because the interviewers will evaluate you every second on your appearance and on how you present yourself.

8. **Eat lightly before the interview.** Eat energy-producing foods. Avoid going to an interview hungry or lethargic.

The Interview Day

It is your interview day. You have worked hard preparing your resume and other materials, contacting people, and practicing for this day. You feel great! You feel confident and prepared! You take one last look at your portfolio presentation and then head for the interview site.

You look at your watch when you arrive. You have exactly 18 minutes before the interview begins. Suddenly, a twinge of nervousness invades your stomach. That is okay. It means that you are a person who cares about doing his or her best.

A few minutes later, someone calls your name. You focus and see a person walking toward you. You stand. You know that you are looking fantastic in your business attire. You are poised and relaxed. The man introduces himself to you as one of the interviewers. He leads you to a conference room where two other interviewers are waiting. With your portfolio presentation in your hand, you walk confidently into the room. Each person says "Hello" and reaches to shake your hand. With a business smile on your face, you extend your hand to each individual and respond with a warm "Hello."

The lead interviewer motions for you to sit in the chair at the head of the table. You sit as directed and place your portfolio on the table in front of you. After the lead interviewer gives a few introductory remarks, he turns to you. He says, "Let me begin this interview by asking you to tell us why you feel qualified for the substitute teaching position that we have available." For a split second you think, "This interview is going to be a piece of cake!"

You open your portfolio and begin. "Let me answer your question by showing ..."

After the Interview

Here are a few things to do **immediately after** you return home from your interview:

1. **Reflect on your interview experience while it is still clear in your mind.** Write down your thoughts and feelings. Reflect on your overall performance. Give special attention to the skills that you performed well. List those skills that you feel you will need to improve before you interview again. Then, list the action steps that you will take at this point to improve.

2. **Write a "Thank you for the opportunity to interview" note to the interviewers.** Briefly, restate how your interest and experience qualify you for the substitute teaching position.

3. **Wait patiently.** During the interview, the lead interviewer told you that he would contact you within five business days regarding the interview team's decision. You may contact the lead interviewer only if you have not received an official call or written notification from him or her by the end of the fifth business day. Until then, it is fingernail-biting time.

How to Become a Highly Sought-After Substitute Teacher

Congratulations! You received the substitute teaching position that you interviewed for several days ago. Now, what can you do to make certain that the principal of the school and the coordinator of the substitute teacher program think of you first when they need a substitute? Here are a few tips to help you move to the top of the "call" list.

- **Be professional.** I offered this suggestion earlier in this book. It is important that you look professional, act professional, and *be* professional in all that you do and say, when you interact with students, teachers, parents, and school administrators.
- **Prepare carefully for every substitute teaching experience.** Never walk into a classroom unprepared. Always have a lesson plan to teach. The plan is either the regular teacher's lesson or one that you develop.

- **Teach with passion.** Never hesitate to let your exuberance show in the classroom. Always give your best.
- **Maintain a positive attitude about the students, staff, and school.** Whenever you hear someone in the school or community make a comment that appears to deride a student, a group of students, the staff, or the school, counter the comment with a positive statement. Whether you are in the staff' lounge or in the local supermarket, always accentuate the positive. As a substitute teacher, you are a member of the school "family." You should feel compelled to speak up.
- **Attend after-school functions.** Show your support and interest in students and staff by attending after-school activities. These events will also provide you with multiple opportunities to enhance your working relationship with everyone in the school.
- **Ask the school principal for permission to attend staff meetings, curriculum development workshops, and instructional training activities.** You will gain an enormous amount of information and training in these sessions that will bolster your confidence and performance in the classroom.
- **Be available to substitute teach.** The person (e.g., principal, substitute teacher program coordinator, Human Resources Director) in the school district who is in charge of contacting substitutes will call reliable and dependable substitute teachers to work. Even in school districts with automated calling system, principals and teachers still want only the substitutes they can count on to come to their schools and perform well in the classroom. If you want to become a highly sought-after substitute teacher in a school district, accept an assignment when the staff person or the automated system calls unless, of course, you have an emergency.

Additionally, plan to be available to work every school day. Do not plan, for example, to work only two days a week, or only on every third Tuesday and Thursday. It is highly unlikely that school administrators will be able to accommodate you with this kind of work schedule.

- **Work cooperatively with staff.** Schools are looking for people who can be team players. They are interested in people who know how to work well with others to get the job done. Look for "little" ways to help, and then, *volunteer* your services. For example, you arrive at an after-school meeting a few minutes early and see two staff people placing packets of materials on tables. Two other people are preparing a table of refreshments. Here is a great opportunity to help. On another occasion, you overhear the vice principal mention that a third-grade teacher had to leave school, suddenly, a few minutes earlier. School will end for the day within thirty minutes. He needs someone to assume the teacher's end of school duty by standing at the door, in the third-grade pod, to supervise the teacher's students as they get on their busses. You do not have an assigned duty at the end of the day. Here is another opportunity to help.

Chapter 2

Characteristics of Successful Substitute Teachers

To waken interest and kindle enthusiasm is the sure way
to teach easily and successfully.
-Tryon Edwards (1809-1894)

If you could ask hundreds of students, teachers, school administrators, and parents what they believe are characteristics of successful substitute teachers, what do you think would be the *consensus* among all groups? I gave you a few clues in Chapter 1. List below what you believe they would say.

Consensus: Characteristics of Successful Substitute Teachers

_____

_____

_____

_____

_____

_____

_____

_____

Here is what I think the consensus would be among students, teachers, and school administrators regarding the characteristics of successful substitute teachers.

They all would agree that successful substitute teachers are

- Pleasant
- Kind
- Caring
- Cheerful
- Patient
- Encouraging
- Helpful
- Friendly
- Respectful
- Polite
- Confident
- Prepared
- Knowledgeable (of subject matter, teaching strategies, student learning styles, emergency procedures, school policies, and so on)
- Flexible
- Resourceful
- Effective classroom managers
- Good disciplinarians
- Able to teach the lesson as instructed
- Punctual
- Professional

What do we agree the consensus would be regarding the characteristics of successful substitute teachers? Place a check mark next to any of the items above that both of us listed.

In addition to the personal and professional qualities that we have listed, successful substitute teachers also have a passion for teaching. They are enthusiastic. Everyone around them can sense their love for children, in all they say and do. They believe all students can learn if given the time, material, and support. They are organized and prepared, encouraging, and affirming. In every aspect of their work, these substitutes convey to students, teachers, principals, and other staff that they are in the school to **teach.**

What Principals and Teachers Expect of Substitute Teachers

Quite often, the personal and professional **characteristics** that students, teachers, school administrators, and parents consider important for successful substitute teachers to have are the same qualities that school principals frequently cite as **their expectations** of substitutes. Talk to public school principals and you will probably hear these comments: "I expect substitute teachers in my school to maintain discipline in the classroom." "I want substitutes to teach the teacher's lesson plan." "I want substitute teachers who like children and want to be with children." "I expect substitute teachers to be on time for school." "I want substitute teachers who have a good rapport with students and staff."

When you teach in a particular school, you will be **required to assume specific roles and responsibilities that are based, primarily, on (a) the school and district polices and procedures, and (b) the building-level administrator's expectations of substitute teachers.** How you perform certain duties in one school may not be the way that you will perform them in another school in the same district. In School A, for example, a teacher leaves instructions for her kindergarten students to form a line a specific way to go to the cafeteria for lunch. In School B, the instructions the kindergarten teacher leaves for his students to form a line to go to the cafeteria are quite different from the directions that the teacher in School A left for her children. At one middle school, you teach reading strategies in math classes because all teachers in that building, regardless of subject area, incorporate reading activities into their lesson plans. In another middle school, in the same district, only the integrated language arts teachers teach reading strategies. The principal of one high school tells you to stand at your door to observe students as they pass in the hallway between classes and at the same time monitor your students as they enter your classroom. In another high school in the district, the principal asks you to be in the classroom as students enter.

Always know what building-level principals and classroom teachers expect of you in their schools. Also, remain flexible and adaptable because each substitute teaching experience is different, and as a result, you will need to adjust to the way "things are done" in the school that you are serving.

The culminating activity to this chapter on the following page will help you determine how the personal and professional characteristics that you have match with the expectations principals and teachers will have of you in their schools. Use the results from the exercise to help you identify your strengths as well as areas you may want to improve.

Exercise: Creating a Personal and Professional Profile

Directions to the Substitute Teacher:

Return to the list of **successful characteristics of substitute teachers** that we developed earlier in this chapter. Which personal and professional qualities from the list do you think you possess? List them below. Add others, if you wish.

Personal and Professional Characteristics

_____   _____

_____   _____

_____   _____

_____   _____

What personal and professional characteristics do you think the principals and teachers of the schools where you want to substitute will **expect** you to have? List those characteristics below. Add others as you think of them

Principals' and Teachers' Expectations

_____   _____

_____   _____

_____   _____

Review the characteristics that you listed and the expectations you think principals and teachers will have of you in their schools. To what extent are the two lists similar? How are they different? Write your answer below.

_____

_____

_____

Chapter 3

How to Prepare for the Substitute Teaching Experience

Failing to plan is a plan to fail.
-Effie Jones

Thorough planning is essential to a successful substitute teaching experience. During the planning process, the substitute teacher gathers as much information as needed about the substitute teaching assignment from the regular classroom teacher, the principal, the program coordinator, and others in the school.

When the School or the Substitute Teacher Locator Contacts You at Least One Day in Advance to Substitute

When the school or the substitute teacher locator contacts you at least one day in advance to substitute teach, visit the school or call the teacher to discuss the lesson plans that you are to teach, the classroom rules and procedures that you are to implement, and the special duties that you are to perform. By the end of your conversation with the classroom teacher, you should know the following:

Background Information

- The name of the teacher for whom you will be substituting
- The class subject (e.g., Math 222, Applied Calculus, Integrated Language Arts, Advanced Placement Spanish, Introduction to Art)
- The grade level
- The time the class starts and ends
- Where the class meets (room number and directions to the room)
- Names of student helpers the teacher has assigned to assist you during class
- Names and duties of educational aides in the classroom
- Names and room numbers of support teachers at the same grade level or in the same department who can provide assistance

- Names of administrative staff and support personnel who can provide immediate assistance and the procedure you should follow to contact them (e.g., principal, vice principal, substitute teacher program coordinator, office secretary, nurse, counselor, and custodian)
- Names of students who have special needs (e.g., inclusion students; students on behavioral modification plans; students who need to visit the nurse's office to take medication; students with special medical conditions such as asthma or diabetes) and a description of each special need
- Classroom rules and procedures (e.g., entering the room, leaving the room during class, lunch, breaks, transitioning from one activity to another in the classroom, sharpening pencils, collecting and distributing materials, working independently, working in teams)
- Dismissal procedures (e.g., end of class, end of day, leaving the room to attend special programs)
- Emergency response procedures (e.g., fire drills, lock downs)
- Teaching materials and equipment required for the lesson (e.g., lesson plan, class roster, seating chart, activity sheets, computer discs, textbooks, workbooks, computers, television, overhead projector, DVD player)
- Location of materials and equipment

Class Activities

A. Beginning of Class: Opening Tasks

- How you will begin class
- The administrative tasks you will complete (e.g., lunch count, attendance)
- The amount of time you should take (in minutes) to complete the "opening tasks"

B. Opening Instructional Activities

- The title of the day's lesson
- The warm-up activity that you will use to focus students' attention on the lesson
- The lesson goals and objectives
- How you will communicate the lesson goals and objectives to students
- How you will check students' understanding of the goals and objectives for the lesson

C. Core Learning Activities

- How you will teach the core learning activities and the procedures you will use to achieve the lesson goals and objectives
- How you will check students' understanding of the lesson
- How you will know if students have learned what you have taught

D. Closing Instructional Activities

- How you will end the lesson and link what students have learned to the lesson that will follow

E. Special Duties

- The extra duties you will perform during the day (e.g., cafeteria duty, hall duty)

F. End of the Day Tasks

- The tasks you will complete at the end of the teaching day for the classroom teacher, the principal, the substitute teacher program coordinator, and others in the school

If you are unable to contact the classroom teacher for whom you will substitute, call the school principal or the coordinator of the substitute teacher program for the information you need for the classes you will teach. If the principal or the program coordinator cannot provide the information that you need, ask for the name of another teacher who may be able to help. This person may be the department/grade level chairperson, or another teacher who is in the same department or who teaches the same subject at the grade level.

Always walk into a classroom **prepared** to substitute teach. For meaningful learning to occur in the classroom, the substitute teacher must be knowledgeable of the day's lesson plan, materials, and tools. You can only teach if you know *what* to teach, *whom* to teach, and *how* to teach.

A sample copy of the Substitute Teacher Planning Log, containing the information discussed in this chapter is on the following page. This log and other materials, products, and supplies are available from Avenegg, Inc. Visit our Website at http://www.aveneggincpublishing.com.

The Substitute Teacher Planning Log

To the Substitute Teacher:

Use this log to take notes and record your ideas as you plan your substitute teaching experience. Use this form as you talk with the teacher for whom you will substitute, to gather information about the class and the lesson that you will teach. Complete the "Personal Reflections" section at the end of your substitute teaching day.

Background Information

Date of Substitute Teaching Experience_____

School _____

Substitute's Name_____ Teacher's Name _____

Class Subject _____ Grade____ Time: From_____ To _____

Room Number_____ Directions to Room _____

Student Helpers _____

Educational Aide _____

The aide will perform the following duties at the times indicated
_____

Support Teachers and Room Numbers (teachers who can provide assistance)
_____
_____

Names of Administrative Staff and Support Personnel and How to Contact Them (e.g., persons who can provide immediate assistance: principal, vice principal, substitute teacher program coordinator, nurse, counselor, secretary, custodian) _____
_____
_____

Classroom Rules and Procedures
_____
_____

Dismissal Procedures

_____

_____

Emergency Response Procedures (e.g., fire drills, lock downs)

_____

_____

Teaching Materials and Equipment (e.g., lesson plan, class roster, seating chart, activity sheets, computer discs, textbooks, workbooks, computers, television, overhead projector, DVD player)

Materials	Location
_____	_____
_____	_____
_____	_____
_____	_____

Equipment	Location
_____	_____
_____	_____
_____	_____
_____	_____
_____	_____
_____	_____
_____	_____

Class Activities

As you complete this section, fill in the TA (Time Allocated for each activity) to help you pace the lesson more efficiently.

A. Beginning of Class

TA _____ Opening Tasks
I will
· introduce myself
· explain, briefly, why the teacher is absent and when he or she is expected to return
· complete administrative tasks (e.g., take the lunch count, check attendance)
· other tasks (Specify) _____

B. Opening Instructional Activities
   TA _____ Warm-Up (An activity to focus students' attention on learning and to prepare them for the day's lesson)

   I will use the warm-up activity listed below to focus students' attention on learning and prepare them for the core instructional activities that will follow.

   _____
   _____
   _____

   TA _____ Core Learning Goals (What students will know and be able to demonstrate at the end of the lesson)

   I will review with students the following learning goals and procedures for achieving those goals.

   _____
   _____
   _____

   TA _____ Checking for Understanding (Feedback: To determine to what extent students know and understand the core learning goals for the lesson and the procedures the class will follow to achieve the goals)

   I will do the following to check students' understanding of the core learning goals and the procedures the class will follow to achieve the goals.

   _____
   _____
   _____

   If students understand the goals and procedures, I will

   _____

   If students do not understand the goals and procedures, I will

   _____

C. Core Learning Activities (The lesson activities that students will engage in to enhance their knowledge and understanding of the core learning goals)

   TA _____ Activity 1 _____
   _____

Procedure _____

_____

TA _____ Activity 2 _____

Procedure _____

_____

TA _____ Activity 3 _____

Procedure _____

_____

D. Closing Instructional Activity (The activity I will use to wrap up the day's lesson and link it to the next lesson)

TA _____ Activity _____

Procedure _____

_____

E. End of the Day Tasks (housekeeping tasks; administrative tasks)

TA _____ I will complete the following tasks for the teacher.

_____

TA _____ I will complete the following tasks for the principal, substitute teacher program coordinator, or others in the school.

_____

F. Personal Reflections (My review of the day's experience)

Here are my thoughts regarding today's substitute teaching experience _____

_____

If I had to teach the same lesson again to the same group of students under the same conditions, I would

_____

_____

The following three words best describe my overall performance today: _____

_____

When the School or the Substitute Teacher Locator Calls You the Morning of Your Substitute Teaching Experience

Quite frequently, school personnel will contact you early on the morning they need you to substitute, because one or more teachers have notified the school that they are ill, a family member is sick, or another emergency has occurred. In these kinds of situations, the person contacting you will ask that you report to school as soon as possible. How do you prepare for this kind of substitute teaching experience, or do you prepare at all? Should you not rush to the school and into the classroom? I encourage you to always plan, even in these circumstances. Here are a few suggestions to help you organize your day:

- **Arrive at school as early as possible.** Sign in and get your identification badge. Notify the person who is responsible for substitute teachers in the building that you have arrived to work. The person in charge can vary from school to school. This individual may be the building-level principal, the vice principal, or the coordinator of the substitute teacher program. In many schools, an office secretary is the person in charge of coordinating substitute teaching services and is the person to contact when you arrive to work.
- **Request from the person in charge a copy of the teacher's lesson plan, the class roster, the seating chart, the school schedule for the day, and the keys to the classroom.**
  First, review the lesson plan carefully. Make certain you have all the teaching materials and equipment that you will need for class. Ask questions if you do not understand certain teaching concepts, strategies, or directions mentioned in the plan. Again, the principal, vice principal, a buddy teacher, or another teacher in the same subject area or at the same grade level can help you.
- If school has not started for the day, **review the teacher's lesson plan** in the classroom. In the classroom environment, you can develop a mind-set and a readiness for teaching as you prepare for the day. Check the instructional equipment that you will use to make certain it is operating properly. Rearrange desks, if necessary, according to the directions the teacher left in the lesson plan. Count textbooks or handouts and match the number that you have with the number that you will need. Obtain additional copies of textbooks and materials, if necessary.
- **Organize the instructional items** that you will use during the lesson. Place workbooks, materials, and supplies in an accessible area of the room. Searching the classroom or sending students to the office for materials or equipment after class has begun wastes

valuable instructional time that students could be actively engaged in meaningful learning experiences.

- Next, **place the class roster and the seating chart side-by-side.** Read a name on the roster and then locate on the seating chart where that student will sit in the classroom. **Memorize the names and seating arrangements for six to eight students.** Remember the names of the four students who will sit at the four corners of the room and of three or four students who will sit in the middle section of the room. During class, make a concerted effort to learn the remaining names of students. Study the following configurations. Circle the letters of students whose names you will memorize *before class* begins and draw a square around the letters of students whose names you will memorize *during class.*

Desks in Rows

A	H	E	J	B
M	K	F	I	L
C	G			D

Desk-to-Desk Student Pairing

F, D	E, I		H, A	
J, C		B, G		

Students Seated at Tables

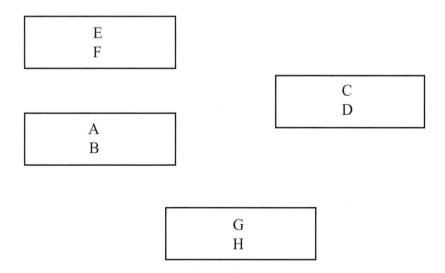

Learn to pronounce the names of all students correctly. If in doubt, ask another teacher. I will say more in Chapter 6 about the importance of knowing and pronouncing students' name correctly.

- Then, **review the school schedule for the day**. Daily schedules do not always remain the same every day in some schools. There are "A" days and "B" days; there are modified "A" days and "B" days and "compressed days" to accommodate various school activities and events. Know the adjustments the school has made for the day. You would probably feel very embarrassed trying to explain to the principal that 21 now crying, hungry kindergartners missed having their lunch because you did not know the bell schedule had changed for the day.

- **Ask the substitute teacher program coordinator about special duties and responsibilities** that you are to assume for the classroom teacher. These duties might include things such as monitoring the cafeteria, bathrooms, halls, or playgrounds at specific times of the day. Make a list of the duties and the times you are to perform them.

- **Inquire about students with special needs who are in the class and how you are to handle each situation.** For example, are there students in the class who have hearing or vision impairments? Are any students on prescription medications? Do any students in class have asthma, seizures, or other medical conditions? Are any students on behavior modification plans? What are the plans and who is involved in the implementation? Finally, ask what attention you are to give each special needs student.

- **Review the appropriate procedures for handling major discipline problems** that could occur in the classroom, reporting those incidents, and assisting students.

- **Inquire about the procedures you and the class are to follow in the event of a schoolwide emergency.** Ask about code words school administrators may use or procedures they may follow in those situations to alert staff of specific emergencies.

- **Request a school map. Take a brief tour of the school.** Learn the locations of the areas that your students will visit during the day such as the cafeteria, library media center, restrooms, gymnasium and playground. Also, pay close attention to the primary exits and alternate exits that your students will use if they have to evacuate the building. Mark areas on your map that you need to remember. If school has started when you arrive, still take time to review the teacher's lesson plan and carefully prepare for the experience. If students are in class waiting for you, there is a staff person in the classroom with them; the person will remain there until you arrive. Again, walk into the classroom "prepared" to teach.

How to Prepare for Your Substitute Teaching Day When You Do Not Have the Teacher's Lesson Plan to Teach

In nearly every professional development session with substitute teachers, several participants tell me that they have substituted, on numerous occasions, in various schools that did not provide them with lesson plans. After listening to their frustrations, I usually say to the group, "So, what is the problem? Simply open *your binder* of lesson plans that *you* have prepared for these kinds of situations and choose appropriate fillers." In Chapter 4, you will learn what fillers are and how to develop and teach them.

What Is in Your Bag?

To begin preparing for those situations when you may not have the teacher's lesson plan, purchase a super-size tote bag. This bag is your *Instructional Materials and Supplies Tote* (IMaST). Fill your bag with general supplies, age-appropriate books, learning activities and other items that will help you have an exceptionally good substitute teaching experience. Always keep your bag packed and ready to go. Here are a few "tools of the trade" that you should have in your bag for every experience.

- The Substitute Teacher Planning Log (a supply)
- The Substitute Teacher Organizer (a supply)
- Pencils (No. 2, already sharpened)
- Erasers
- Ballpoint pens (red, black, and blue)
- Highlighters (a variety of colors)
- Transparency markers
- Magic markers
- Crayons
- Rulers (at least two)
- Paper clips
- Stapler (filled with staples)
- Scissors
- Tape (Scotch tape and masking tape)
- 3x5 note cards
- 5x8 note cards
- Post-its
- Stickers
- Motivational certificates
- Chalk
- Board eraser
- Blank transparencies
- Notebook paper

I Come to Teach!

- File folders or pocket portfolios
- Dictionary
- Construction paper
- Timer
- Nametags
- Help tents
- Tissues
- Large print picture books (grade-appropriate, pre-k through elementary)
- Books (high-interest books for middle and high school students)
- Fillers (meaningful learning activities that substitutes can teach for a few minutes or an entire class period)
- Grade-appropriate children songs
- Small rubber ball
- Flashcards
- Brain games
- Stuffed animals or puppets

Also carry the following emergency-response items in your IMaST:

- Vinyl or latex gloves (At least 2 pairs)
- Antiseptic pads
- Instant antiseptic hand cleanser
- Cell phone

Carry your **IMaST** with you every time you teach. When students see you with your big bag, they will *assume* that you take substitute teaching seriously; that you have planned for the day; and that teaching, doing, and learning most likely will occur that class period. Your tote, alone, will do much to change the attitudes of those students who think they will "have a day off" because they have a substitute teacher.

The Substitute Teacher Organizer

In addition to completing *The Substitute Teacher Planning Log,* you will also need to do a *zillion* other things to adequately prepare and remain organized during the substitute teaching experience. How will you remember everything that you will need to do? You can make a list or use *The Substitute Teacher Organizer* below for this purpose.

The Substitute Teacher Organizer

General Preparation: *Before* You Arrive at School

Use this checklist to help you remember the things that you need to do to plan and manage your substitute teaching experience. Check an item after you complete it, and provide comments, if needed, in the space provided below the statement. Add items at the end of the section.

Before You Arrive at School

☐ Obtain the name and location of the school where you will be substitute teaching.

_____

☐ Ask the substitute teacher program coordinator the time school starts.

_____

☐ Ask the substitute teacher coordinator the time that you should report to school.

_____

☐ Ask the substitute teacher program coordinator the name of the teacher that you will be substituting for and the date.

_____

☐ Ask the substitute teacher program coordinator the grade level and subject that you will teach.

_____

☐ Request a copy of the teacher's lesson plan from the coordinator of the substitute teacher program.

_____

☐ Complete **The Substitute Teacher Planning Log.**

_____

☐ Pack your **Instructional Materials and Supplies Tote (IMaST)** with grade-appropriate activities and supplies.

_____

☐ Prepare a transparency of five or six classroom rules and procedures.

_____

☐ Review the school's discipline policy and place a copy in your **IMaST.**

_____

☐ Review the school's emergency drill procedures and place a copy in your **IMaST.**

_____

☐ Place a copy of **The Substitute Teacher Organizer** in your **IMaST.**

_____

☐ Dress appropriately on the day of your substitute teaching experience.

_____

☐ Become enthusiastic, confident, and ready for the day.

_____

☐ Smile.

_____

☐ Become physically, mentally and emotionally ready to "**teach**."

_____

Additional Things I Need to Remember

☐

_____

☐

_____

☐

_____

☐

_____

General Preparation: At School Prior to the First Class

Use this checklist to help you remember the things that you need to do to plan and manage your substitute teaching experience. Check the item after you complete it, and provide comments, if needed, in the space provided below the statement. Add items at the end of the section.

Prior to your first class

☐ Arrive at school **at least 45 minutes before** your first class begins. If school is in session, arrive as soon as you can.

_____

☐ Report to the office, sign in, and inform the principal or the substitute teaching program coordinator that you have arrived.

_____

☐ Request and review a copy of the day's bell schedule.

_____

☐ Request a copy of the teacher's lesson plan if you did not receive a copy prior to arriving at school.

_____

☐ Review the teacher's lesson plan and ask questions about the things you do not understand.

_____

☐ Review the teacher's class rules and procedures.

_____

☐ Review the school policy regarding students' use of cell phones, pagers, the school phones, and so on.

_____

☐ Locate textbooks, supplies, and other materials you need for class.

_____

☐ Learn how to operate the equipment that you will use in class.

_____

☐ Learn the names of special needs students who will be in your class, and the accommodations that you will make in the lesson you teach.

_____

☐ Learn the names of the student helpers who will be in your class, and the kind of assistance they are to provide.

_____

☐ Become familiar with the areas of the school and grounds (cafeteria, computer center, playground, library media center) that your students will use during the school day.

_____

☐ Review the teacher's class roster and seating chart.

_____

☐ Learn how to pronounce correctly the names of all students on the teacher's class roster, and memorize the names of at least six students on the seating chart.

_____

☐ Learn how to report student attendance.

_____

☐ Review the school's emergency alert drills and procedures that your students and you are to follow.

_____

☐ Know how and when to contact the office administrators, school counselors, school nurse, custodian, and other staff members for assistance.

_____

☐ Learn the names of teachers in the general area of the classroom, and introduce yourself to them.

_____

☐ Obtain a list of the extra duties (e.g., cafeteria, hall, playground) that you are to perform, and when you are to perform them.

_____

☐ Obtain the keys to the classroom.

_____

☐ Write your name on the chalkboard, including a phonetic spelling.

_____

☐ Write the teacher's warm-up activity and lesson objectives on the chalkboard, or prepare the information to show on an overhead or LCD projector.

_____

☐ Place on the overhead or LCD projector the tasks that you want students to complete as soon as they enter the classroom, to prepare for the day's lesson.

_____

☐ Check all of the equipment that you need for the day's lesson to make sure it is working properly.

_____

☐ Check textbooks, supplies, handouts, and other support materials to make sure everything is readily accessible.

_____

☐ Make certain that you have the correct number of handouts, other materials, and supplies that you need for students.

_____

☐ Develop a procedure for distributing and collecting class materials and supplies.

_____

☐ Review how to perform administrative tasks (e.g., lunch count, attendance) quickly and efficiently at the beginning of class.

_____

☐ Review the **fillers** that you plan to teach or use as back-up activities.

_____

☐ Arrange students' desks for the day's lesson.

_____

Additional Things I Need to Remember

☐

_____

☐

_____

As Students Enter the Classroom

Use this checklist to help you remember the things that you need to do to plan and manage your substitute teaching experience. Check the item after you complete it, and provide comments, if needed, in the space provided below the statement. Add items at the end of the section.

As students enter the classroom

☐ Stand near or at the door or some other designated place.

_____

☐ Smile and greet students.

_____

☐ Model for students the behaviors that you want them to exhibit in class. Show students through your body language and words that you are pleasant, polite, courteous, respectful, and confident.

_____

☐ Monitor students' interactions as they prepare for class.

_____

Additional Things I Need to Remember

☐

_____

☐

_____

During Instructional Time

Use this checklist to help you remember the things that you need to do to plan and manage your substitute teaching experience. Check the item after you complete it, and provide comments, if needed, in the space provided below the statement. Add items at the end of the section.

When the bell rings

☐ Walk purposefully into the room immediately after the bell rings to begin class.

_____

☐ Stand at the front of the room, or at some strategic focal point in the room, to begin class.

_____

☐ Look alive and be vivacious! Convey to student through your demeanor that you **are there to teach.**

_____

☐ Use direction-focused strategies to get students' attention.

_____

☐ Greet the class.

_____

☐ Tell students who you are, why you are there, why their regular teacher is absent, and when they can expect him or her to return.

_____

☐ Complete administrative tasks quickly and efficiently, while students complete their warm-up activity.

_____

☐ Give students the day's lesson objectives.

_____

☐ Give students the learning activities for the day, why and how they will be engaged in the tasks, and what they should know and be able to do at the end of the lesson.

_____

☐ Check students' understanding of the lesson objectives and the procedures they are to follow to complete their assignments.

_____

☐ Assist students as they work independently and in cooperative cohorts.

_____

☐ Keep learning activities "moving." Avoid "down time."

_____

☐ Make smooth transitions between activities.

_____

☐ Address student behavioral problems immediately.

_____

☐ Involve students in a wrap-up of the day's activities by reviewing key points of the lesson, giving students their homework assignment, and previewing the following day's lesson.

_____

Additional Things I Need to Remember

☐

_____

☐

_____

Near the End of Class

Use this checklist to help you remember the things that you need to do to plan and manage your substitute teaching experience. Check the item after you complete it, and provide comments, if needed, in the space provided below the statement. Add items at the end of the section.

Near the end of class

☐ Have students perform "housekeeping" tasks, such as logging off computers and returning materials and supplies to the appropriate places.

☐ Give students specific directions for leaving the room at the end of class.

☐ Close the day with words that inspire and encourage students.

☐ Listen carefully to students' comments regarding the lesson.

Additional Things I Need to Remember

☐

☐

After the Last Class

Use this checklist to help you remember the things that you need to do to plan and manage your substitute teaching experience. Check the item after you complete it, and provide comments, if needed, in the space provided below the statement. Add items at the end of the section.

After your last class

☐ Write a brief summary of the day's activities for the teacher.

_____

☐ Return all instructional materials, supplies, and equipment to their appropriate places.

_____

☐ Complete all housekeeping tasks (e.g., remove paper from the floor; clean the chalkboard)

_____

☐ Complete all administrative tasks as instructed.

_____

☐ Reflect on your substitute teaching experience.

_____

☐ Close the classroom door gently as you leave.

_____

☐ Celebrate!

_____

Chapter 4

Planning and Teaching Fillers

Plan your work for today and every day, then work your plan.
-Norman Vincent Peale (1898-1993)

What can you do after you have taught the teacher's lesson plan and you still have five, ten, or twenty minutes of extra time before class officially ends? What can you do when you arrive at school and learn that the teacher did not leave lesson plans or the plans cannot be located? Consider using the "fillers" that you developed earlier for these situations. **They are in your Instructional Materials and Supplies Tote (IMaST).**

What are Fillers?

Fillers are meaningful educational activities that you can use when you do not have the teacher's lesson plan, or after you have taught the lesson plan and you have a few minutes left in the class period.

Where Can You Find Fillers?

Educational journals and books are excellent sources to use to find fillers or ideas for fillers. You may find a selection of journals, books, and materials on the professional shelf or in electronic form in the school library media center. Browse dollar stores; these are businesses that sell each item for one dollar. You should be able to find an assortment of age-appropriate children's books and other educational materials. Visit educational supply stores, and you will find everything from A to Z for substitute teachers.

Educational games such as *Brain Quest* are great fillers. You may be able to purchase these games at Toys R Us, Sam's Club, Wal-Mart, or other stores that carry educational supplies. Zillions of fillers and ideas are available at a variety of educational sites on the Internet. Before you begin using the information, talk to a school library media specialist or a technology specialist about copyright laws governing the use of materials on the Internet for educational purposes.

Ask your children for ideas that would be most appropriate for their age and grade level. Share your plans with them as you work. Your children will have fun helping you with your homework.

Use your creative mind to develop fillers. Think of fun ideas and high-interest activities that students will enjoy and benefit from educationally. Then, think of the expertise that you have in those areas of interests. For example, you may have traveled extensively in the United States or abroad to places that many students may never have an opportunity to visit. How can you develop fillers from these experiences? Do you have pictures? Can you take students on a pictorial journey? Can you share tips and strategies on taking an award-winning photograph with a digital camera?

A substitute teacher who was in a course that I taught several years ago at a community college had a passion for designing fish ponds. Since she was working as a long-term substitute teacher at a local middle school, this substitute developed a miniunit of lessons that she could use with students over several days. The lessons centered on two or three essential core learning goals in math and science for that grade level. She incorporated vocabulary and spelling activities into the lessons, along with reading, writing, speaking, and listening skills. She provided students opportunities to work independently and in teams. At the end of the miniunit, each student had a personal design that the family could use to construct a fish pond at home.

On the next several pages are three, easy-to-teach fillers. The first two activities will take approximately 30 minutes to teach. The third filler will take three or more days to teach; this activity is more appropriate for a long-term substitute to use until the regular teacher's lesson plans become available.

Sample Fillers

Filler 1: Higher Order Thinking and Problem-Solving

(Appropriate for students of Grades 6-12)

Give every two students in class a new, unsharpened, No. 2 pencil and one 8 ½ x 11 sheet of construction paper. (Use the same style and brand of pencils for this activity.) Working together, the two students are to determine how many pencils they will need to lay side-to-side to cover only a 7½ x 10 area of the construction paper. The two students are to list on paper the steps they follow to solve the problem, review their steps for clarity and accuracy, and present their findings orally to the class.

Getting the correct answer is important. Equally important are the steps the students take to arrive at their answer and how well they work cooperatively to solve the problem.

At the end of the activity, give everyone a new, unsharpened, No. 2 pencil as a reward.

Filler 2: Future-Thinker

(Appropriate for Grades 4 -12)

Write the following sentence starter on the chalkboard or on the overhead projector:

I want to...

Ask students to respond in writing. They are to explain
- What **goal** they want to achieve
- Why it is important to them
- What they will do to achieve the goal
- When they expect to reach their goal
- How achieving their goal will benefit them and others

Students are to write complete sentences and use their best writing skills. Tell students that you will also respond in writing to the sentence starter as they write. If they should have questions or need assistance after they begin the activity, they are to place their "Help Tent" (a folded 5 x 8 index card, with the word "Help" written on it) on their desk and continue working. You will assist them at their desks.

When everyone finishes the activity, give students the **Listening for Details** handout. Here is a sample form.

Listening for Details

Student's Name	Goal	Why Goal Is Important	What to Do to Achieve Goal	When Expect to Reach Goal	How Will Benefit Self	How Will Benefit Others

Project a copy of the same handout on the overhead projector. Ask for student volunteers to read to the class what they have written. As a student reads, the class listens for the details in the handout. When the student finishes reading, the class fills in the "Listening for Details" section, indicating the student's goal and so forth. Then, engage students in a discussion of the details they have heard, and record that information on the overhead projector. After everyone, including you, has an opportunity to share aloud his or her goal and you have recorded the information on the overhead, ask the class to look for similarities and differences in the details. For example, are two or more students interested in the same goal? Do any students have different goals but similar approaches to achieving them? Involve every student in the discussion.

I Come to Teach!

Filler 3: What a Great Idea!

(Appropriate for Grades 4 -12)

Place a familiar object that is commonly used every day (e.g., pencil, pen, eraser, or straw) in a paper bag. Prepare one bag for every two students in class. The two students are learning partners and will work together to complete the activity.

To begin, the learning partners select a paper bag. They are to "reinvent" the item they have chosen. For example, a pencil is no longer a pencil. They are to create a new and different item that is just as useful and beneficial to society. To make the activity more challenging, you may have students reinvent the item for use in a specific field or occupation. For example, you may place in the paper bag with the item a note that instructs the learning partners to reinvent something that can be used in a particular area (e.g., sports medicine, automotive industry, marine biology, computer technology), or by a person in a specific occupation (e.g., nurse, engineer, ballet dancer, country/rock star).

In the culminating activity, students present their "reinventions" to the class along with the materials they develop. Encourage students to give computer-generated presentations or use transparencies, large posters, or other visuals. Give learning partners ten minutes to present and an additional five minutes to answer questions from the class.

Give the learning partners guidelines for completing the activity. Consider the following suggestions:

1. **Decide** what your reinvention will be and how it will be helpful to society to have your reinvention. Determine if your reinvention is most beneficial to particular age groups or types of people. Write your ideas down on paper.
2. **Name** your reinvention.
3. **Describe** your reinvention on paper. How does it look? How does it sound? What can it do? What is its texture? **Describe** your invention with such clarity that a third-grade student will be able to pick out your reinvention in a group of others, based on what you have written.
4. **Make** a black-and-white sketch of your reinvention on an 8 ½x11 sheet of construction paper.
5. **Explain** how your reinvention works. List the steps in the process on the following graphic organizer:

Graphic Organizer: Our Reinvention

Learning Partners: _____ and _____

Name of Our Reinvention: _____

This is how our reinvention works. Explain the process below.

Step 1 First,

_____

_____

Step 2 Then,

_____

_____

Step 3 Next,

_____

_____

Step 4 Finally,

_____

_____

6. **Pull it all together**. Go back to numbers 1, 2, and 5. Review your notes from these activities Use the information from the activities as an outline to write a paper about your reinvention. Use your best writing skills.

7. **Determine** whether you need to patent your reinvention. Use a classroom computer or visit the library media center to do a little **research**. Gather as much information as you think you need to make a decision; however, in your search, be sure to find information about the purpose of a patent, how you can obtain one, and the requirements, procedures, and cost.

8. **Sell! Sell!** You have decided that your reinvention is a good product to sell. Do you need a business license or a special permit to mass market your item? Contact the appropriate local government agencies for information. First, list on paper the questions you will ask the agency's representative when you call.

9. **Advertise**. Now, you are ready to let people know that your "reinvention" is for sale. Complete two of the following activities:

- Develop an ad for the local newspaper.

- Develop a 30-second TV commercial.

- Write and set to music a 30-second jingle for the radio.

- Develop a flier.

- Design business cards to distribute.

- Develop a PowerPoint presentation to give to the local Chamber of Commerce.

- Other: _____ (Learning Partners' Choice)

10. **Prepare materials and rehearse** the presentation that you will give to the class.

What a Great Idea! Guidelines for Presentations

Establish and discuss with students the procedures for giving their oral presentations to the class. For example, you may decide that the learning partners should

- Stand at the front of the room to give their presentations

- Speak so everyone in the class can hear them

- Maintain good eye contact with the class

Give the other students in class the handout on the next page, *Presentations of Reinventions.* Have students record their thoughts about the reinventions and the learning partners' presentations. Discuss with students how and when they are to complete the handout.

Have the class applaud the learning partners after they give their presentations. Ask for student volunteers to share aloud what they liked most about the reinvention or the presentation.

Collect the handouts from students at the end of each presentation. Give the learning partners the completed handouts regarding their presentation, after you have reviewed them.

What a Great Idea!

Presentations of Reinventions

Learning partners: _____

Original item: _____

Name of reinvention: _____

Description of reinvention: _____
_____
_____

What I learned about the reinvention: _____
_____
_____
_____
_____

What I like most about the reinvention: _____
_____
_____
_____

Here are my suggestions for improving the reinvention: _____
_____
_____
_____

This is what I liked most about your presentation: _____
_____
_____
_____

This is how I think you can improve your next presentation: _____
_____
_____
_____

After All Students Have Presented

First, provide time for the learning partners to review the handouts they receive from the class, make desired changes, and revise their projects for publication. Next, have students think of ways they can publish their work. Here are a few suggestions:

- Make a class booklet of students' descriptions and sketches of their reinventions. Duplicate and distribute booklets to other classes.
- Place students' reinventions in a school display case.
- Have students present their reinventions to younger students.
- Display students' work in the classroom.
- Have the class select (by paper ballot) two sketches of students' reinventions to submit to the school newspaper. Submit the sketches, along with a brief article on each.

Then, have each student think about the project and his or her involvement. Ask students to list on paper what they gained most from the activity and what, if anything, they would do differently, if they were going to do the same project again. Have students share their thoughts with their learning partners. Finally, end the activity with a whole class discussion of students' ideas.

Creating Your Own Filler-Activity

Here is your opportunity to develop a filler that you would like to teach. The activity should take at least 30 minutes to teach. Begin by writing down your ideas on the "Filler Outline Exercise" form on the next page. Then, develop your filler, using the Creative Lesson Planning for Substitute Teachers form on the page after that. Have fun!

Filler Outline Exercise

Directions to the Substitute Teacher: Use this form to develop an outline for a filler-activity that you would like to teach. As you select a topic and complete your outline, carefully **choose age-appropriate and grade level-appropriate topics, themes, and materials for your projects.** When in doubt about what you can and cannot use, discuss your ideas with the school principal.

Think of a topic that you would like to develop. Write it below.

_____

What special interest or expertise do you have in the subject matter?

_____
_____
_____
_____
_____

At which grade level(s) will you use your filler (e.g., Grade 2, Grades 7-8, Grade 10)?

_____

Which subject areas will you focus on in your filler (e.g., social studies, language arts, art, music, etc.)?

_____
_____

How long do you think it will take you to teach your filler (e.g., 30 minutes, 90 minutes)?

_____

Creative Lesson Planning for Substitute Teachers Form

Use this form to prepare a basic, generic lesson plan. Use your plan if the classroom teacher does not leave a lesson plan or other activities for you to teach. **Obtain approval from the school principal or his or her designee before you teach your lesson.**

Lesson Topic _____ Grade _____ Subject _____

Classroom Teacher _____ School _____ Date _____

Subject Linkages _____

Vocabulary Focus _____ Spelling Focus _____

Lesson Overview (Write five or six sentences describing the purpose of your lesson.)

_____
_____
_____
_____
_____
_____

Lesson Objectives (Write three measurable objectives)

At the end of this lesson, students will be able to:

_____
_____
_____

Checking for Understanding (How you will know if students have learned the material and have achieved the lesson objectives by the end of class)

I will know that students have learned the material and have achieved the objectives if students can:

_____
_____
_____
_____

Introducing the Lesson

This is how I will

- get students **interested** in the lesson

_____
_____
_____
_____

- explain to students **what** they will be doing in class that period

_____
_____
_____
_____

- explain to students **how and why** they will be engaged in the lesson activities

_____
_____
_____
_____

- explain to students **how long** it will take them to complete each activity

_____
_____
_____

- explain to students **what they should know and be able to do** by the end of class

_____
_____
_____
_____

Lesson Activities

I will complete the following activities in the order that I have listed them.
Before each activity is the amount of time that I intend to use for this part of
the lesson.

_____ (Time) Activity 1:

_____
_____
_____
_____

_____ (Time) Activity 2:

_____
_____
_____
_____

_____ (Time) Activity 3:

_____
_____
_____
_____

_____ (Time) Activity 4:

_____
_____
_____
_____

Lesson Summary

This is how I will end the lesson:

_____
_____
_____
_____

I Come to Teach!

Materials, Supplies, and Equipment for the Lesson

I will need the following materials, supplies, and equipment to teach the lesson.

Materials	Supplies	Equipment	Other

Approval

❑ **I** approve of (name) _____, the substitute teacher, teaching this lesson in (class) _____, on (date) _____

❑ **I** approve of (name) _____, the substitute teacher, teaching this lesson in (class) _____, on (date) _____ with the following changes to the plan_____

_____

_____

_____

Principal's or Designee's Signature of Approval

_____

Principal or Designee: Please print your name on the line above.

_____

Date

Filler-Activities Log

Keep a record of all the fillers you teach. Write in your notes the title of the filler, the name of the school where you taught the activity, the class and grade level, the name of the teacher for whom you were substitute teaching, and the date you taught the lesson. Additionally, write your overall impression of the lesson you taught, and list any changes that you want to make before you teach the filler again.

Use the sample Filler-Activities Log on the following page as a guide as you develop your record keeping forms. Maintain the list of filler-activities you teach in a computer file. Keep a current copy of the list in your IMaST.

Filler-Activities Log

Filler _____ Date Taught_____

School _____ Teacher _____

Class _____ Grade _____

My Overall Impression of the Filler-Activity I Taught

_____
_____
_____

The Things I Want to Change Before I Teach the Lesson Again

_____
_____
_____

Filler-Activities Log

Filler _____ Date Taught_____

School _____ Teacher _____

Class _____ Grade _____

My Overall Impression of the Filler-Activity I Taught

_____
_____
_____

The Things I Want to Change Before I Teach the Lesson Again

_____
_____
_____

Chapter 5

It Is Time to Teach!

When I approach a child
He inspires in me two sentiments:
Tenderness for what he is,
And respect for what he may become.
-Louis Pasteur (1822-1895)

Suddenly, you feel a twinge of nervousness, but it quickly passes because you know you are prepared for the substitute teaching assignment.

You began planning soon after you received the call yesterday. You have made all the general preparations and have reviewed the regular teacher's lesson plan. At this point, you need to walk around the classroom before the bell rings to make sure you have done everything that is necessary to prepare the classroom and materials for your students' arrival. With ***The Substitute Teacher Organizer*** (see Chapter 3) in your hand, you turn to the section *General Preparation: At School Prior to the First Class* and begin to review the list to make sure you have completed everything.

All items are checked. You are ready for class. Now, take a deep breath and say aloud, convincingly, **"I come to teach!"**

Ring! Ring! Ring! Here they come! Listen! Listen and you will hear locker doors clanging and children laughing and chatting in the halls. How exciting! Here are a few additional suggestions to help you have a great day:

As Students Enter the Classroom

- **As students enter your classroom, stand near or at the door** (unless the principal or the designee directs you to do otherwise). Position yourself so that you are visible and accessible and at the same time, able to monitor the immediate area around your classroom door and in the classroom, simultaneously.

- **Greet students** with a friendly smile and a warm "Hello" as they enter the room.

- **A few students will ask to leave the classroom as soon as they enter for a myriad of reasons.** They will ask your permission to go to various places including the water fountain, the restroom, the office, or to their lockers for forgotten books, homework, pens, pencils, paper, lunch money, and more. Do not allow the *"I want"* and *"I need"* unnerve you. I suggest that you calmly, courteously, and firmly say "No," followed with a reason such as "The bell will soon ring and class will begin with an activity that I know you will not want to miss." If the student persists, again reiterate, "No, I'm sorry; you may not leave the room."

   Now, there are always exceptions to everything. If, for example, the student presents you with an "official" note from the office that states you are to "excuse" him or her at that time, then you would allow the student to leave.

When the Bell Rings

- **Do not linger at the door when the bell rings to begin class,** even if you see a friend walking up the hall toward you. Wave and smile at the person, turn and walk into the classroom, immediately. When you take your first step into the room, begin counting from 1 to 30 silently as you walk because thirty seconds is the amount of time you will have to establish a working relationship with the class. Do not saunter in; rather walk purposefully to the front of the room. In classrooms that do not have a defined "front," find a strategic place in the room where all students can see you, with minimal difficulty. Relax and give the impression that something important and exciting is about to happen in the room. Do not stand behind a podium, table, or any other object that students can perceive as the "great divide" between you and them. Stand in close proximity to students and express in your body language that you are pleased to be with them.

- As you quickly scan the room, you notice that all but two students have already begun the warm-up activity that you had projected on the overhead as students entered the classroom. You overhear one of the two students asking a classmate for a pencil. Look in your **IMaST**, take out a sharpened pencil and give it to the student. Smile. At this point, you may be tempted to make extraneous comments to the student about coming to class unprepared. Do not! Always give students sharpened pencils that have good erasers. If they are unsharpened, students will need to leave their desks to go to the pencil sharpener. Sharpening pencils during instructional time can be very disruptive and a primary cause of discipline problems. Also, give students pens that write well or expect to have them returned to you, immediately, with a few unnecessary comments from students that you probably could have avoided.

  The second student appears to be wandering aimlessly around the room. Establish and maintain eye contact with the "wanderer" and wait quietly for the student to sit and begin work. When the student sits down, smile and give an affirmative nod, and say very softly, "Thank you." At this point, the student will probably begin work. If the student does not begin the warm-up activity immediately, walk over to the student quietly and calmly. Wear your same smile. Without other students overhearing you, ask if he or she needs your assistance to begin the activity. Ask the student if he or she has paper, a pencil or other materials to complete the activity, if you do not see these items on the student's desk. Check to make sure the student understands the directions to the activity. Provide whatever assistance the students needs. Leave the student once he or she successfully begins the activity. Now, walk around the room to make certain all students have begun the warm-up activity successfully.

- Complete administrative duties quickly and efficiently while students are completing the warm-up activity.

- When students complete the warm-up activity, greet the entire class with a friendly "Good morning" or whatever is appropriate for that time of the day. Say those words energetically. Smile. Then give your name. Tell students that you will be their "teacher" for the day or class period:

Good morning! My name is Mrs. Ranksy. I am your teacher for the day.

Continue to wear your smile. If you have a name (e.g., Pig, Grass, etc.) that people have joked about in the past, be assured that a few students in your class will think of other jokes to add to your list. Before they have a chance to share their ideas with the class, tell students one or two funny things that people have said. Show the class that you have a sense of humor.

- Tell students the reason their teacher is absent and when you expect him or her to return. Do not share detailed or confidential information. The principal or the coordinator of the substitute teacher program in the school can tell you what is most appropriate to say.

Teaching the Lesson Plan

- **Begin instructional activities immediately.** Give students the lesson objectives for the day. Write the objectives on the chalkboard before students enter the room or display them on the overhead or LCD projector. If, for some reason, you are unable to write the objectives on the chalkboard or display them on an overhead or an LCD projector, place a copy of them on each student's desk before class begins. The lesson objectives should be visible to students at all times during the period.

    Review the lesson objectives with students. Check their understanding of them. Make certain all students know what they are to do that period, how to do it, and what they will know or will be able to demonstrate by the end of class.

- **Assist student as they work.** As students work independently or in cooperative or collaborative groups, move around the room from student to student and from group to group to provide assistance as needed. Sit with groups and beside individual students as they work independently. When you are in close proximity to students, they are more likely to (a) stay on task, and (b) ask for your help, if they should have difficulty with a learning activity. Additionally, you are better able to coach students as they work, praise students for specific performances, and encourage them to continue when you are near them.

Under no circumstances, should you "perch" on or sit at the teacher's desk and read, or stand in one specific place in the room with your arms folded and simply observe. Be with students in the classroom. Be both engaged and engaging.

- **Handle special concerns and problems discreetly.** A student asks to go to the restroom. This student asked you the same question as he was entering the classroom at the beginning of the period. You told him then that he could not leave the room because the bell was about to ring and class would begin with an activity that you knew he would not want to miss. What should you do, now that the student is asking a second time to go to the restroom? Use your best judgment.

- **Keep learning activities moving at a smooth, steady pace.** Avoid "down time." Whether the lesson is student driven or substitute teacher directed, keep students actively engaged. When students have too much time to complete an activity, they tend to become bored and look for noninstructional things to do such as writing notes, sending text messages, leaning back in their chairs until they rest on two legs, walking aimlessly around the room, taking another student's personal belongings, touching inappropriately, or talking among themselves about personal matters.

  In your effort to avoid down time, make certain that you do not give students *too little time* to complete activities. Students tend to become frustrated and eventually stop working when they feel rushed unnecessarily. In all instructional situations, pacing the lesson effectively is a very important teaching strategy that substitute teachers should give considerable attention.

- **Make transitions between activities quickly and efficiently.** Before making a transition from one activity to another, bring closure to the part of the lesson that the class has just completed. If students have worked on other related activities prior to the one they have just finished, remind them how their completion of the sequence of instructional tasks to this point is helping them to achieve their goals for the day's lesson. Link those tasks to the next activity. Give clear, concise instructions for completing the next activity. Give students models of the tasks they are about to begin, so they can see what their finished products will resemble. Always check students' understanding of directions, procedures, and anticipated learning results before they begin their work. There are many ways to check for understanding. A simple strategy is to call students randomly to orally reflect back to the class the goals, directions, procedures, and anticipated outcomes of the activity.

- Near the **end of the day's lesson,** engage students in a review of key points from the lesson. Return to the goals and reconnect them to the instructional activities that you taught and students learned. In the review process, check students' understanding of the lesson again, and list in your notes areas where reteaching may need to occur.

- **The teacher left homework.** Give students the assignment and review the instructions carefully. Again, check students' understanding of what they are to do and how they are to do it. Provide a few minutes for students to begin the activity, if the materials they need are available in the classroom. Move around the room as students work. Provide students with assistance, and praise them for what they complete well or attempt.

- **Tell the class about the next lesson**. Give students teasers. Give students just enough information to get them interested and excited about the activities that they will engage in next time.

Ending Class

- **Near the end of class, provide time for students to perform housekeeping duties**. Have students, for example, return resource materials to their proper location in the room, remove paper from the floor and inside their desks, log out on their computers, and perform other tasks that are necessary to return the room to a neat, clean, orderly place. If the room was not neat, clean, and orderly when you arrived, your goal, then, is to **leave the room looking better than you found it.**
- To get the housekeeping chores done without creating havoc in the classroom, give students specific instructions for performing each task.

- Near the end of class, give students directions for leaving the classroom when the bell rings. To a middle or high school class, you may say:

When the bell rings, please stand quietly and place your chairs back to your desks. Team number two will leave first, followed by team three, and then team one. Take your scrap paper with you as you leave the room and drop it into the trash can. Thank you.

- Always end class on a positive note. Tell students how much you enjoyed working with them and that you hope the school will call you again to substitute in their class. Also, thank students for their cooperation and assistance. Now, what do you say to that uncooperative class? You did not enjoy working with those students, and you hope the school never calls you again to teach them? As you struggle to think of something positive to say to this class, remember, what you say at that moment may be the only encouraging words those students will hear all day. Think of *something* that students did well in class and praise and thank them for that effort.

The bell rings, ending class. Students leave quietly and orderly. They place all but two chairs back to their desks. Only one piece of scrap paper misses going into the trash can, and that came from a "want to-be-pro-basketball star" that could not resist using a wad of paper to go for the game-winning point.

Two students pause on their way out to tell you that they enjoyed having you for their substitute teacher. Another student mumbles, "You're okay." How well did your day go? Listen to your thoughts and to your heart.

After Your Last Class

After your last class for the day is over and students have left the room

- Complete the **Personal Reflections** section (Section F) in the ***Substitute Teacher Planning Log.***

- **Write the teacher a brief summary of your experience**.
  Include the following information:
  - The class in review: Your overall impression of the class
  - The number of students who attended class
  - Names of students who were absent from class
  - Names of students who were tardy to class
  - Names of students who were dismissed early from class
  - Names of the *awesome students* (These students worked and cooperated well with you and their peers.)
  - Names of the *five-star students* (These students' work was exemplary. Not only did these students complete all of their activities and cooperate well with you and their peers, they also helped other students in class who had difficulty with various aspects of the lesson.)
  - Names of students who were off task and were disciplined for their misbehavior
  - Unusual class occurrences (e.g., verbal or physical altercations)
  - Three things that you liked most about teaching the class
  - Three things that would be most helpful to you next time, if the regular teacher can provide them

On the following page is the form, **Substitute Teacher End of the Day Summary for the Teacher,** which includes all of the above items.

- Place **students' work in a file folder**. Use a separate folder for each class. Give the *Five-Star Students* and the *Awesome Students* certificates of recognition. Place the certificates in the folder for the teacher to hand out when he or she returns to class. Place the folder in the teacher's desk drawer or in another mutually agreed upon place. Also, leave manuals, lesson plans, and a completed copy of the **Substitute Teacher End of the Day Summary for the Teacher.**

- **Complete the Substitute Teacher End of the Day Summary for the Principal.** Give two copies of the completed form to the principal, with one of the two copies designated for the regular teacher. A copy of this form is also included in this chapter.

Substitute Teacher End of the Day
Summary for the Teacher

Directions to the Substitute Teacher: Complete a feedback form for each class, at the end of your day. Place the form in a folder for the teacher, and leave it with the other class information.

Date of the Substitute Teaching Experience _____

School _____

Substitute Teacher_____

Teacher_____

Class _____ Class Time: From _____To _____ Grade_____

The Class in Review: My **overall impression** of the class

_____
_____
_____
_____
_____

Attendance

This is the number of students **who attended class**: _____

These students were **absent from class**:

_____   _____
_____   _____
_____   _____

These students were **tardy to class**:

_____   _____
_____   _____
_____   _____

These students had an official early **dismissal** from class:

_____   _____
_____   _____
_____   _____

I Come to Teach!

Lesson Activities

Here is an overview of the work that we covered in class: _____

_____

_____

_____

We were unable to complete the following activities: _____

_____

_____

Reason: _____

_____

Student Participation and Behavior

Here is a list of the *awesome students* in class. They worked and cooperated
well with their peers and me:

_____   _____

_____   _____

_____   _____

_____   _____

These were the **five-star students** in class. Their work was exemplary. Not
only did these students complete all of their activities and cooperate well with
their peers and me, they also helped other students in class who had
difficulty with various aspects of the lesson.

_____   _____

_____   _____

_____   _____

_____   _____

These students were **uncooperative:**

Student: _____

Problem:

_____

_____

_____

How Problem was Resolved:

_____

_____

_____

Student: _____

    Problem:

_____
_____
_____

    How Problem was Resolved:

_____
_____
_____

The following **unusual class occurrences** (e.g., verbal, physical altercations, etc.) occurred:

    Occurrence:

_____
_____
_____
_____

    How situation was resolved:

_____
_____
_____
_____

The following **unusual class occurrences** (e.g., verbal, physical altercations, etc.) occurred:

    Occurrence:

_____
_____
_____
_____

    How situation was resolved:

_____
_____
_____
_____

I Come to Teach!

Kudos

Here are three things that I **liked most about teaching** your class:

_____
_____
_____

Next Time

The following things would be **helpful next time**, if you can provide them:

_____
_____
_____
_____

Additional Notes to the Regular Teacher

_____
_____
_____
_____

How to Contact Me

Please contact me if you should need additional information:

Telephone (including area code) : _____

The best time to contact me: _____

Email: _____

Substitute Teacher's Signature   _____

Date Submitted   _____

Thank you!

Substitute Teacher End of the Day Summary for the Principal

To the Substitute Teacher: At the end of the day, complete this feedback form for the school principal. Give two copies to the principal, with one copy designated for the regular classroom teacher.

Date of the Substitute Teaching Experience _____

Substitute Teacher_____ School _____

Regular Classroom Teacher _____Class _____ Subject _____

Part I. Planning for the Substitute Teaching Experience

I was provided time to	Circle Answer	
Contact the regular classroom teacher about the substitute teaching experience	Yes	No
Complete my *Substitute Teacher Planning Log*	Yes	No
Review the teacher's lesson plan and related instructional materials, the school schedule for the day, and other information	Yes	No
Locate and set up instructional equipment for the lesson	Yes	No
Ask the regular classroom teacher, the principal or the designee questions before I began the substitute teaching experience	Yes	No

Comments _____

Part II. Substitute Teaching Experience

I was provided an opportunity to	Circle Answer	
Teach from the regular teacher's lesson plan	Yes	No
Teach from my *Substitute Teacher Planning Log*	Yes	No

Seek the assistance I needed throughout the school day from other teachers in the same subject area or grade level, the principal, or the designee	Yes	No
Interact with teachers and other staff members during the day (e.g., cafeteria, staff meetings, special events)	Yes	No
Interact with students during the day in the cafeteria, at special events, or at other nonteaching functions	Yes	No

Comments: _____

Part III. End of the Substitute Teaching Day

I was provided an opportunity at the end of the substitute teaching day to	**Circle Answer**	
Complete all of the end of the day tasks for the teacher and school administrators	Yes	No
Discuss my observation with my observer	Yes	No
Reflect on my substitute teaching experience	Yes	No

Comments: _____

Part IV. Kudos

Here are three things I **liked most about teaching** in the school:

_____
_____
_____

Part V. Next Time

It would be **helpful if the school can provide the following next time:** _____

Substitute Teacher's Signature_____

Date Submitted _____

Thank you!

Chapter 6

Effective Classroom Management and Discipline Strategies

We think of our efficient teachers with a sense of recognition,
but those who touched our humanity we remember with gratitude.
Learning is the essential mineral,
but warmth is the life-element for the child's soul,
no less than for the growing plant.
-Carl Gustav Jung (1875-1961)

This chapter is based on the following *principles* about substitute teaching, classroom management, discipline practices, and student learning in today's classroom:

- The substitute teacher is both a teacher and a learner in the classroom. The student is both a learner and a teacher in the classroom. The substitute teacher and the student have a right to teach and learn in an evironment that is positive, engaging, and free from disruptive behaviors.

- Substitute teachers who effectively plan and organize their teaching experiences are more likely to manage their learning environments more efficiently than their counterparts who fail to plan or fail to plan adequately.

- The substitute teacher is the most influential factor in the classroom. This individual determines what extent students learn and enjoy learning.

Classroom Management Defined

For the purpose of our discussion in this chapter, **classroom management** includes everything that a substitute teacher does in the classroom to make certain effective teaching and student learning occur. To manage a classroom well, the substitute teacher must be able to

- Plan and organize instructional materials

- Teach the classroom teacher's lesson plan or self-prepared fillers

- Attend to administrative matters in the classroom quickly and efficiently

- Operate instructional equipment in the classroom, with minimal assistance

- Arrange student seating and materials in the classroom to maximize student interaction and learning

- Create and maintain a positive and engaging learning environment

- Implement school and classroom rules and procedures

- Encourage appropriate student behavior

- Manage inappropriate student behavior

- Assess the students' performance and his or her own performance in the classroom to determine what extent effective teaching and learning occurred.

Discipline Defined

Discipline is a key element of classroom management. It includes everything a substitute teacher does in the classroom to **turn an inappropriate student behavior into an appropriate behavior, and then, maintain that behavior so he or she can teach and students can learn.** To achieve this end, the substitute must be able to use various **classroom rules and procedures** that the school and the classroom teacher have preestablished for this purpose.

The **rules** in the classroom are *what* students *(and the substitute)* follow to facilitate the teaching and learning process. The **procedures** are *how* students (and the substitute) carry out the rules. For example, School A has a *rule* that a student who is late for class must obtain a "late-to-class note" before he or she enters the classroom. The *procedure* requires the student who is late for class to first report to the office and then give the vice principal the reason he or she is late for class. The vice principal decides whether the reason is acceptable or unacceptable and then gives the student an excused or an unexcused late-to-class note. Upon entering the classroom, the student gives the note to the substitute teacher who then indicates in his or her class log the notation: *excused* or *unexcused*. In many situations, students know and understand class rules but have little, if any, understanding of the procedures for successfully implementing those rules. In the School A example, a student may know to report to the office for a late note, but does not know that he or she is to talk to the vice principal about the situation. Additionally, instead of giving the substitute teacher the obtained note upon entering the classroom, the student sits at his or her desk and waits for the substitute teacher to ask. As a result, other problems, including discipline problems, are likely to emerge from this one circumstance because the student does not fully understand school or class procedures. It is important that substitute teachers know the established rules and procedures and carry them out accordingly.

Classroom management and classroom discipline are highly interrelated. The substitute teacher who is an effective classroom manager is more likely to have fewer discipline problems than a substitute who is unable to manage. When discipline problems occur in the classroom, the substitute should first determine how well he or she is managing the learning environment. Here are nine key questions the substitute can ask himself:

- How well do my students understand their class assignment?
- Am I giving students enough, but not too much, time to complete learning activities?
- Do students know what to do after they finish an assignment?
- Do students understand the class rules and procedures for working independently and cooperatively in teams?
- Am I monitoring students as they work?
- Am I assisting students when they need my help?
- Am I minimizing class disruptions when I hand out and collect students' papers and materials?
- Am I redirecting off-task students to their assignments as soon as I observe their misbehavior?
- Am I positive, encouraging, and supportive?

To become effective classroom managers, substitute teachers can begin by

- Examining their management/discipline style and the factors that influence their practices
- Understanding what students want in a learning environment, and what can occur when those *wants* go unmet
- Understanding practical management and discipline strategies that can promote successful teaching and learning

Let us look more closely at each area.

Exercise: What Is Your Management/Discipline Style?

Directions to the Substitute: Complete the following activity.

Part A. Complete the following sentence. Write what comes first to your mind.

1. What do you think is your management/discipline style in the classroom? (e.g., democratic, laissez-faire, autocratic)? Explain.

   _____

   _____

   _____

2. If I asked the person who knows you best to describe you, what six adjectives would the person use? List those words below.

   _____   _____

   _____   _____

   _____   _____

3. How did your parents manage/discipline you as a child?

   _____

   _____

4. Think of a K-12 teacher who taught you in school. What was this teacher's management/discipline style?

   _____

   _____

5. What is your management/discipline style at home?

   _____

   _____

Part B. Read the following statements. Place a check mark in the column, *Yes* or *No*, that best represents your answer.

	Yes	No
I invite my children, grandchildren, and others in the home to participate in home management decisions.	_____	_____
I *encourage* my children, grandchildren, and others to express themselves freely in the home.	_____	_____

I *listen* to others when they speak by stopping what I am doing, by giving and maintaining good eye contact with the person, and by occasionally reflecting back to the individual what I hear.   _____ _____

I *ask* rather then *tell* others to do specific things.   _____ _____

I *use* courtesy words such as *please* and *thank you*.   _____ _____

I gently care for my pets.   _____ _____

I accentuate the positive qualities that I see in others.   _____ _____

I accept my children and spouse or partner as they are with an understanding that they are still *becoming* as individuals.   _____ _____

I set parameters in the home for my children or grandchildren.   _____ _____

I can say "no" to others at home without feeling guilty.   _____ _____

Part C. Complete the summary activity.

Review your answers to numbers 2, 3, and 4 in Part A. What similarities or differences do you find in the answers you gave? For example, did you write that your parents and your teacher were **indulgent**? Did you write that the person who knows you best would describe you as a **kind, understanding, and accepting** person? Notice the similarities in the responses you wrote.

_____
_____
_____
_____
_____
_____
_____
_____
_____
_____

Part D. Review your answers to number 5 in Part A. How is your response to this question similar (or different) to your response to questions 2, 3, and 4?

_____
_____
_____
_____
_____

Part E. Finally, based on the answers you gave in Parts A through D of this exercise, how do you think your parents, your teacher, and your current management and discipline style at home have influenced **your management/discipline style in the classroom**?

_____
_____
_____
_____
_____

What Students Want and Expect from Substitute Teachers

Quite often young people have difficulty explaining to others what they *need,* but they seldom have problems stating what they *want.* I believe there are several things students *want* from their substitute teachers. First and foremost, students want you to **teach**. They want you to either teach the regular teacher's lesson plan or provide them with meaningful activities that you have prepared for class. Students do not want "a day off," as they sometimes ask for when they enter the room. Above all, they do not want you to waste their time in the classroom because you are not prepared or are underprepared.

Students want you to respect them and model the behavior in the classroom that you want them to exhibit before you and the class. Begin by pronouncing students' names correctly or showing the class that you are seriously trying. Attempt to know the first name of every student in class before the period or day is over. Announce to students at the beginning of class that one of your personal goals for the day is to learn their first names.

Additionally, when you have a request of a student, include the word *please* in the sentence. When the student completes what you have requested, immediately follow up with the words *thank you.* You can also use the words *thank you* along with the word *please* as you request something of a student. For example, you might say, "Marty, *please* help me distribute these workbooks. *Thank you.*" You are implying that you know Marty is willing to help; therefore, you are thanking him or her in advance. You can also say *please* and *thank you* when you request something of the entire class. *Please* and *thank you* are very soothing and thoughtful words that usually generate positive responses.

Students want to feel physically, mentally, socially and emotionally safe in the classroom. In addition to knowing the school policy for handling various emergencies, the substitute teacher can help to ensure the safety of children in the classroom by providing a positive and encouraging learning environment, where all students can learn and become socially responsible citizens, without fear of harassments and putdowns. To help students feel safe in the classroom, create a climate where students can freely take academic risks and give their best. Promote an atmosphere where students value healthy competition but honor teamwork. When a student teases, bullies, threatens, or does other things that make it difficult for his or her peers to function in the classroom, deal with the situation quickly and discreetly.

Exceptionally quiet students in class want your personalized attention. The quiet students can be, for the most part, the *invisible* students in your classroom. They seldom misbehave. Usually, these students work well independently but do not function as well in groups. They can be passive learners who, at times, appear to feel more comfortable observing the learning process as it develops around them than actively participating in it. These students can also appear aloof. They do not have class friends. They may sit alone when they eat in the cafeteria. Frequently, they are vulnerable to the more assertive or aggressive students and can eventually become targets of their pranks and jokes. If left unattended, the *invisible* students can become your in-class "drop outs."

Seek out the exceptionally quiet students in your class:

- Ask yourself the proverbial question, "What do these students want from their peers and me in this classroom that we are not providing?"

- Encourage quiet students to express their thoughts and concerns. Listen carefully to what they say, without being judgmental.

- Make certain they have multiple opportunities to experience success in the classroom.

- Praise students for their performance.

Usually, students want to know how they will benefit now and in the immediate future from what they are about to learn or are learning. They want to be able to connect the dots between *personal benefit* and *class activity*. If there is a close match between the two entities, students will give considerable thought and effort to completing the assigned tasks. If students perceive only a remote connection or no connection between *personal benefit* and *class activity*, they will give little or no effort to completing their work. In other words, a fourth-grader will not necessarily understand the "benefit" she can derive from learning how to do fractions because you tell her that she will need the information when she is an adult. On the other hand, if you place a real or a construction paper model of a pizza in front of her, and give her the responsibility of dividing it equally for herself and three of her classmates, suddenly she sees the "personal benefit" that she can receive from the learning activity.

How to Handle Students' "Wants" in the Classroom

Students engage in disruptive behavior in the classroom to get the attention of their peers and the substitute teacher when the substitute does not provide for their basic *wants*, as they *expected*.

For example, a student who does not read well may refuse to work independently to complete an activity. He may try to disguise his inability to read the material by saying to you, "I'm not doing this stuff. Why do we have to do this, anyway?" If you insist without recognizing that the student has an underlying *want*, which, in this situation, is to be able to read in order to complete the assignment, the student will continue to be disruptive. He may purposefully distract other students in class by calling out to them, throwing paper, writing notes, or walking around the room. This student may also show his lack of interest in the lesson by doodling on paper or by putting his head down on the desk and falling asleep while other students work.

One way you can address this problem is to help the disruptive student successfully begin the activity. You can work one-on-one with the student to help him understand the directions to the activity. Read part of the directions aloud with him, and then have him continue. You or the educational aide in the classroom can spend additional time working one-on-one with the student during the period, until he successfully completes the assignment.

When a student is disruptive in the classroom, do not *assume* that the child simply wants to be obstinate. Rather, ask yourself, "What does this student *want* in this classroom from his or her peers and me that we are not providing?" Then, do everything possible to address those "wants."

Practical Management and Discipline Strategies That Promote Teaching and Learning

Substitute teachers should make certain students understand class rules and procedures. In some classrooms, the regular teacher posts the rules and procedures on the wall or another conspicuous place. Review those and other rules for the day at the beginning of the lesson and then again during the lesson, as needed. Make sure students understand not only the rules but also the procedures and the purpose for having them. Periodically, randomly call students to reflect back to the class key points that they are to remember from the discussion. Finally, ask all students who are willing to "ratify" and "carry out" the rules and procedures of the day to raise their hands. If some students are reluctant to raise their hands, ask them to share with the class which rule or procedure they do not agree with and why. Students who will not openly show their acceptance of classroom rules and procedures will probably cause some disruption to the class later.

If the classroom teacher does not leave specific rules and procedures for the day, establish your own and communicate them to students. Focus on three or four essential rules and procedures; do not overwhelm students with a long list of dos and don'ts. Remain flexible so that you can always add to your list or modify what you have prepared as the teaching day progresses. When preparing your list, ask yourself these two questions: (a) How will the rules and procedures promote teaching and learning? (b) How will the rules and procedures help to provide what students *want* in class from their peers and me?

As you and students discuss the rules and procedures for the day, it is also important to talk about what the consequences will be if infractions should occur. For minor infractions, consider giving the student who breaks the rule two opportunities to correct the misbehavior, with assistance from you and other students, if needed. When the misbehavior first occurs, give the student a gentle warning and remind him or her of what the acceptable behavior is for that given situation. Remind the student of the consequence if he or she chooses to misbehave again as well as the reward, if any, for exhibiting the desired behavior. This conversation is a one-on-one discussion with the student. The entire class should only be involved with a discipline issue when all or a majority of the students in class are responsible for having committed the infraction. If the student chooses to misbehave again, he or she should receive the full consequence for the action.

Consider the **Class Rules, Procedures, and Consequences Planner on the next page.** This tool can help you prepare for this management aspect of your substitute teaching experience.

Class Rules, Procedures, and Consequences Planner

Directions to the substitute teacher: As you plan your substitute teaching experience, determine which items below will best support the lesson that you will be teaching. Place a check mark beside the number(s) of the item(s) below that you will discuss with the class. Write in the space under each item the rule, procedure, and consequence for infractions. Give each student a copy of the checklist with the information. Students are to circle the item number as you discuss them in class.

Remember to ask yourself the following two questions as you prepare your checklist and discuss the items with the class:

- How will the rules and procedures promote teaching and learning?

- How will the rules and procedures help me provide what students *want* in class from their peers and me?

Items

1. _____ Entering the classroom
Rule: _____
Procedure: _____
Consequences for infractions: _____
_____
_____

2. _____ Leaving the classroom
Rule: _____
Procedure: _____
Consequences for infractions: _____
_____
_____

3. _____ Returning to the classroom
Rule: _____
Procedure: _____
Consequences for infractions: _____
_____
_____

4. _____ Beginning of class routine

Rule: _____

Procedure: _____

Consequences for infractions: _____

_____

_____

5. _____ Out-of-seat activities in class

Rule: _____

Procedure: _____

Consequences for infractions: _____

_____

_____

6. _____ Whole class participation

Rule: _____

Procedure: _____

Consequences for infractions: _____

_____

_____

7. _____ Group work

Rule: _____

Procedure: _____

Consequences for infractions: _____

_____

_____

8. _____ Individual participation in group work

Rule: _____

Procedure: _____

Consequences for infractions: _____

_____

_____

9. _____ Independent work

Rule: _____

Procedure: _____

Consequences for infractions: _____

_____

_____

10. _____ Peer assistance with class work

Rule: _____

Procedure: _____

Consequences for infractions: _____

_____

_____

11. _____ Taking a test

Rule: _____

Procedure: _____

Consequences for infractions: _____

_____

_____

12. _____ What to do after completing an assignment

Rule: _____

Procedure: _____

Consequences for infractions: _____

_____

_____

13. _____ Distributing class materials and supplies

Rule: _____

Procedure: _____

Consequences for infractions: _____

_____

_____

14. _____ Collecting class materials and supplies

Rule: _____

Procedure: _____

Consequences for infractions: _____

_____

_____

15. _____ Homework

Rule: _____

Procedure: _____

Consequences for infractions: _____

_____

_____

16. _____ Using the pencil sharpener
Rule: _____
Procedure: _____
Consequences for infractions: _____
_____
_____

17. _____ Using the drinking fountain
Rule: _____
Procedure: _____
Consequences for infractions: _____
_____
_____

18. _____ Eating in the classroom
Rule: _____
Procedure: _____
Consequences for infractions: _____
_____
_____

19. _____ Engaging in personal conversations in class
Rule: _____
Procedure: _____
Consequences for infractions: _____
_____
_____

20. _____ Using the teacher's desk
Rule: _____
Procedure: _____
Consequences for infractions: _____
_____
_____

21. _____ Using your desk and other students' desks
Rule: _____
Procedure: _____
Consequences for infractions: _____
_____
_____

22. _____ Using class equipment
Rule: _____
Procedure: _____
Consequences for infractions: _____
_____
_____

23. _____ Using cell phones, pagers, and other personal
electronic devices
Rule: _____
Procedure: _____
Consequences for infractions: _____
_____
_____

24. _____ Using the trash can
Rule: _____
Procedure: _____
Consequences for infractions: _____
_____
_____

25. _____ End of class routine
Rule: _____
Procedure: _____
Consequences for infractions: _____
_____
_____

26. _____ (Other)
Rule: _____
Procedure: _____
Consequences for infractions: _____
_____
_____

27. _____ (Other)
Rule: _____
Procedure: _____
Consequences for infractions: _____
_____
_____

How to Prepare and Teach a Minilesson on Classroom Rules and Procedures

Long-term substitute teachers who have the responsibility for developing lesson plans should consider teaching a minilesson concerning classroom rules and procedures at the beginning of their long-term experience. The purpose of the lesson would be to (a) involve students in determining the rules and procedures they consider important for class, and (b) provide students with opportunities to demonstrate an understanding of those rules and procedures.

Here is a **sample minilesson** on classroom rules and procedures.

Lesson Objectives: At the end of the minilesson, students will be able to
- name three classroom rules and procedures
- demonstrate an understanding of the three classroom rules and procedures

Primary Instructional Strategies:
- Think/Team/Share
- Whole Class Activity

Lesson Activities:

Independent Student Activity (Two Minutes)
> First, ask students to think of **five** different places or events where people are required to follow specific rules and procedures. Then, ask students to think why it is important for those people to follow these rules at those places or events. Have students write their ideas on paper.

Team Activity (Two Minutes)
> Form student teams. Randomly assign four students to each group.

Team Activity (Four minutes)
> In groups, students are to share their lists of rules and procedures and tell why they are important. During the discussion, students may add ideas to their lists. The group should select at least three rules and procedures to share with the whole class.

Team/Whole Class Activity (Five Minutes)
- Randomly call a student from each team to share a rule and procedure and the reason the team felt it was important.
- List rules and procedures on the overhead or chalkboard as students share them aloud with the class.
- Ask the class to look at the list for places and events that have similar rules and procedures.

Team Activity (Six Minutes)

Give each student a classroom rule and procedure on a sheet of paper. All members of a team are to receive the same rule. Students are not to look at the rule and procedure until you say the word, "Look." When you tell them to look, students will have three minutes to work quickly listing reasons why the classroom rule and procedure on their paper is important.

Then yell, "Look!"

Team/Whole Class Activity (Six Minutes)

- Randomly call a student from each team to share with the class the rule and procedure the team received, and then tell why the rule and procedure are important.

- Continue until the class discusses all of the rules and procedures. Near the end of the class discussion, tell students that in this activity, they identified the rules and procedures for their class. Project a complete list of the rules and procedures on the overhead. At this point, establish with students a working definition of the terms "rule" and "procedure." Post the definition on the Classroom Rules and Procedures wall, along with their papers.

- Call on students to summarize key points from the lesson.

- At the end of the activity, make a Classroom Rules and Procedures wall. Post students' papers on the wall. Recognize each team for its work. Give a special recognition to the top ten individual students and the top three teams with the highest number of *reasons why their classroom rules and procedures are important.*

- Thank students for their input. End the activity.

Exercise: Preparing and Teaching a Minilesson
on Classroom Rules and Procedures

Using the sample lesson plan format on the previous two pages or the sample format provided in Chapter 4, develop a minilesson on classroom rules and procedures that you can actually teach.

To help you get started, use the space below to jot down ideas for your minilesson. You are on your own from this point forward. Get the creative juices flowing!

Ideas for My Minilesson

_____

_____

_____

_____

_____

_____

_____

How to Praise and Encourage Positive Student Behavior

Students tend to perform better in class when they receive praise and encouragement. Discipline problems are minimal, if they occur at all. For example, you say to Renee, before a third-grade class of her peers, "I like the way you have followed directions so well. You have two sheets of paper and a storybook on your desk. You are looking at me. You appear prepared for the next activity. Thank you, Renee." Suddenly, other students will begin placing their paper and storybooks on their desks. As you see these students exhibiting the behavior you want, acknowledge them by saying something like, "Thank you, Philees. You have two sheets of paper and a storybook on your desk. You are looking at me. You are also ready for the next activity." Within a few seconds, the entire class will be ready to work.

Praise and encourage students' performance as they work independently, in teams, or as a class. Praise students with words or with tangible rewards. Here are a few sample sentences and sentence starters that praise and encourage students:

- I like the way ...

- I really appreciate ...

- What a great idea!

- What an interesting way to look at ...That's something we [the class] had not considered.

- You have almost solved the problem. You have ... Keep working.

- That ...is awesome. It has ...

- This team has worked together exceptionally well. The group has ...

- I am so proud of the way this class ...

- Thank you for ...

- You have worked so hard to ...

Tangible rewards can include
- Recognition certificates
- Pencils
- Erasers
- Stickers
- Free ice cream coupons
- Lunch with the substitute teacher in the cafeteria
- Educational activities (e.g., games, crafts, discussion groups)

The message is this:

- Accentuate the positive things students say and do in the classroom
- Encourage the student who sincerely *tries* to solve a problem in an activity as well as the child who answers every problem correctly
- Provide a classroom environment where students feel comfortable, valued, and affirmed

Engage students in these and other similar activities in the classroom. Eventually, disruptive students will understand that the *best* way to gain attention from their peers and their substitute teacher is to exhibit positive classroom behaviors that win them praise, encouragement, and acceptance; these are the three things students *want most,* and perhaps crave, in the classroom.

In the activity on the following page (or on a separate sheet of paper), list ways that you can praise and encourage students in the classroom. Make a list of sentence starters that you can use. Then, add to the list the names of several items that you can give students as rewards. Before giving the rewards, ask the classroom teacher or the school principal if you can use tangible rewards in the classroom to reinforce positive behavior; and if you can, the kinds of rewards that would be most appropriate.

How I Can Praise and Encourage Positive Student Behavior in the Classroom

Here is what I can do in the classroom:

Sentence Starters

_____

_____

_____

_____

_____

_____

Tangible Rewards (Before giving students stickers, pencils, or other rewards for positive performance in the classroom, always check with the classroom teacher or the school principal to make certain the school permits the use of items for this purpose.)

_____

_____

_____

Other Ways I Can Praise and Encourage Positive Student Behavior

_____

_____

_____

Teaching Students How to Recognize and Celebrate their Everyday Successes

Quite often, students focus so intently on achieving what they consider their "big" goals in life that they overlook the importance of their daily accomplishments. As a result, young people frequently miss opportunities to recognize, celebrate, and enjoy the successes they experience every day.

Here is an interesting little activity that you can teach to help students understand the concept of success and the significance of celebrating everyday achievements:

> Have each student list on paper a personal goal that he or she wants to achieve. For example, a student may want a special date for a school dance. Another student may want to gain admission to a specific Ivy-League college.
>
> Then, ask students to list all of the things they have done that day (or week or month) to take them one step closer to their goal. As students write their lists, make certain they also focus on the things that they often overlook and take for granted. For example, they chose to get out of bed that day to attend school. Once at school, they chose to attend their classes. Perhaps a student passed a difficult test earlier that day. Another student works part-time after school and, at the same time, maintains an A average. These accomplishments should be recognized and celebrated because they would be unable to achieve their goals, if they chose not to attend school or classes on too many school days.
>
> After they create their lists, ask student volunteers to share aloud with the class one or two items from their lists. When students share an item, they are to "pat themselves" on the back and say celebratory statements (e.g., Great job! Awesome! I did exceptionally well!). Students will have fun doing this exercise, and at the same time realize that they are achieving some notable things every day.

Monitoring Your Own Attitude and Behavior

Throughout this chapter, I have emphasized how critical it is for a substitute teacher to

- Thoroughly plan for the teaching experience
- Know his or her management style
- Meet students' basic "wants" in the classroom
- Establish and communicate rules and procedures to students
- Praise and encourage positive student behavior

It is also critical that you are aware of your personal feelings, attitudes, and perceptions about students, substitute teaching, and the learning process. Your feelings and attitudes shape your perceptions. Your perceptions greatly determine your actions and behaviors in the classroom.

As you complete the following exercise, think about the importance of monitoring your own feelings, attitudes, and perceptions in the classroom, and the impact of it all on teaching and learning.

Part A. Read the following words or group of words. Write in the space provided after each what comes *first* to your mind.

- At-risk students

  _____
  _____
  _____

- Talented and gifted students

  _____
  _____
  _____

- On free and reduced lunch

  _____
  _____
  _____

I Come to Teach!

- High performers

  _____
  _____
  _____

- Basketball team

  _____
  _____
  _____

- Low achievers

  _____
  _____
  _____

- Golf team

  _____
  _____
  _____

- Level IV students

  _____
  _____
  _____

- Remedial Math I students

  _____
  _____
  _____

  Christie

  _____
  _____
  _____

  Harriet

  _____
  _____
  _____

Part B. Review

- What images of students came to your mind as you read each word or group of words?

  _____

  _____

  _____

  _____

- Did you associate students of a particular race, gender, ethnicity or economic status with certain words? If your answer is _yes_, explain.

  _____

  _____

  _____

  _____

- How can your mind's images and preconceived thoughts, feelings, and attitudes about students influence the way you teach?

  _____

  _____

  _____

  _____

I Come to Teach!

As I was leaving a business luncheon with a colleague, at a local restaurant a man approached me. I recognized him as a former student from years past but could not recall his name. Immediately, he began to tell us how another educator and I, in the school district where I had worked, had been his "role models." During our conversation, he frequently repeated how I had encouraged and inspired him in the classroom to do his best. According to this young man, he owned, at the time, several successful, prominent communication franchises nationwide.

Always pay careful attention to the feelings, attitudes, and behaviors that you exhibit in the classroom. Be aware of what you say and how you say it. Choose your words carefully, and express them gently. Monitor *yourself* at all times, because the sentiments and opinions that you express or do not express can greatly determine the extent students learn and succeed.

Chapter 7

Managing Student Behavior in the Classroom

I am the decisive element in my classroom. It is my personal approach that creates the climate. It is my daily mood that makes the weather. As a teacher, I possess tremendous power to make a child's life miserable or joyous. I can be a tool of torture or an instrument of inspiration. I can humiliate or humor, hurt or heal. In all situations it is my response that decides whether a crisis will be escalated or de-escalated, a child humanized or de-humanized.
-Haim Ginott

Managing student behavior can be a daunting task for the most experienced substitute teachers. For many substitutes, trying to keep students on task, and at the same time, dealing with disruptive behaviors can be stressful and time-consuming. "It takes away from valuable class time," says one substitute in a workshop. "Why can't students come to school understanding the purpose for school and schooling?"

Managing Appropriate Student Behavior in the Classroom

What could be more exhilarating for you than to have a group of students who know and understand the class rules and procedures? They are attentive and on task during the period. They complete their independent assignments as you had intended, and they work exceptionally well and cooperatively in teams. They are pleasant, polite, and self-motivated.

How do you encourage and maintain this kind of appropriate student behavior in the classroom? Here are a few tips worth remembering:

- Keep all students actively engaged in the lesson, from the beginning to the end of class. Avoid "down time." During this "time," students have nothing constructive to do or are unclear about what to do next.
- Create and maintain a positive classroom climate, where every student feels valued, safe, connected, and successful.
- Monitor student behavior.

- Be among students as they work so that you can coach, facilitate, question, probe, praise, encourage, and inspire.
- Teach! Teach! Teach with passion!

Managing Inappropriate Student Behavior

Students in your next class talk excessively when they should be working independently or completing group activities. Some call out to their peers across the room. Several students walk around the classroom continually socializing, while others eat food without permission, chat idly, or pass notes. They constantly tease and "put down" each other. What could be more exasperating for you? What can you do?

First, focus on ways to prevent this kind of inappropriate student behavior from occurring in your classroom. Again, consider the suggestions that I just gave on ways to maintain appropriate behavior in the classroom. Here is the list again.

- Keep all students actively engaged in the lesson, from the beginning of the period to the end. Avoid "down time." During this "time," students have nothing constructive to do or are unclear about what to do next.
- Create and maintain a positive classroom climate, where every student feels valued, safe, connected, and successful.
- Monitor student behavior.
- Be among students as they work so you can coach, facilitate, question, probe, praise, encourage, and inspire.
- Teach! Teach! Teach with passion!

Also, review Chapter 5, "It Is Time to Teach!" The first question that you will probably want to ask yourself when problems occur in the classroom is, "What does the student, who is causing the disruption, want in this classroom that I am not providing?" The second question you will want to ask is "What instructional changes do I need to make to better accommodate the student's wants and needs in this classroom?"

Additionally, consider the following strategies:

- Attend to a disruptive student immediately. Do not ignore the behavioral problem, even if it is a minor distraction, because the student will probably continue to exhibit the inappropriate behavior. Your primary goal in this situation is to stop the misbehavior before it becomes contagious and spreads throughout the entire class.

- Involve only the student or students causing the disruption in your effort to correct the problem. Try to continue class activities as you deal with the situation. Only involve the class when the entire class or a vast majority of the students are disruptive.

Managing Minor Inappropriate Student Behavior

Specifically, when dealing with **minor behavioral problems** (e.g., idle chatter, passing notes, eating):

- Establish and maintain eye contact for a few seconds with the student who is off task. This is not a "stare-down." You should look serious but nonintimidating. The look should convey this message to the student: "I need your attention. I need you on task, now." If the student stops the inappropriate behavior and returns to work, continue what you were doing, but monitor the student's behavior throughout the remainder of the period.

- Establish and maintain eye contact with the student again if he or she becomes disruptive again. Walk slowly, quietly, and gently over to the student. Do not appear aggressive or confrontational. Once in close proximity, wait a few seconds for the student to redirect his or her attention to the class activity. If the student appears unsure of the task he or she should be completing, provide assistance until the student is able to continue without your help. Again, monitor the student's behavior.

- Establish and maintain eye contact with the student again if he or she should become disruptive for a third time. Again, walk slowly, quietly, and gently over to the student. Do not appear aggressive or confrontational. Once in close proximity, ask the student how you can help him or her successfully stay on task. Remember, you are talking quietly and privately to the student. Other members of the class should not overhear the conversation, except, perhaps, for the student who is sitting next to the disruptive student.

   If the student asks for assistance from you or another student, provide that help. If the student shrugs his or her shoulders or gives a flippant remark, restate in one sentence the task the student should be completing. Begin your sentence with the person's name. You may say something similar to the following statement: "Chris, you should be working on problem number four, on page 262." In a follow-up statement, give Chris an *I Message* that includes what you perceive to be the disruptive behavior, how it affects others in the class, and what you "need" him or her to do, as a result. Here is a sample *I Message*:

> Chris, when you rock your chair back and forth on two legs, your classmates around you stop working to watch you. I need you to put your chair down, now, on all four legs, keep it down, and begin problem number four, on page 262.

At this point, attempt to get a commitment from Chris. Ask Chris if he or she will agree to your request: "Will you do, now, what I have asked?" Pause. Give the student a few seconds to respond, and make the transition from "chair-rocking" to "problem-solving." If the student says "Yes" to your request, thank the student for being cooperative. Then, ask how you can help him or her with problem number four, on page 262. If needed, provide assistance until the student is able to proceed independently.

What can you do if Chris' reply is "No," to your request? In one simple sentence, calmly remind Chris of the class rule, which relates to "chair-rocking" or general, off-task behaviors, that the class discussed at the beginning of the period. Then, remind the student of the "consequence" for that infraction, which was also discussed. Next, follow through by administering the "consequence."

Here are two things that you definitely want to **avoid doing** when working with disruptive students:

- Avoid lecturing or interrogating the student with remarks such as: *This is the second time I have asked you to stop rocking your chair on two legs! Chris, what part of my sentence do you not understand? What are you supposed to be doing? Why can you not do your work like the other students in this class? You will get a big, fat zero for today, if you do not have your work completed by the end of this period, if you are still in this room at the end of this period.*

- Do not be confrontational in what you say or do. Do not walk toward a disruptive student hastily and aggressively. Avoid raising your voice or sounding angry when you speak. Avoid pointing your finger at the student or flailing your arms. Be in proximity to the student when you speak, but do not invade the student's personal, physical space. Do not give ultimatums.

- Avoid appearing indecisive to students when you explain the actions you plan to take to resolve the behavioral problem. Decide on your course of action before you begin, but remain flexible as you proceed so that you can adapt to the situation as it develops. Then, follow through.

Managing Major Inappropriate Student Behavior

Major disruptions frequently occur in the classroom when students are allowed to make rude remarks to other students or to the substitute teacher, call other students (or the substitute) inappropriate names, tease or put down their peers, engage in inappropriate gesturing, or hit or push students. These and other similar behaviors that are intended to hurt another person in the classroom physically, mentally, or emotionally are unacceptable and should be dealt with swiftly and directly.

The students who are not participating in these events in class will expect the substitute teacher to handle these and other behavioral problems appropriately, and not ignore them.

Every situation is different, and you must do what you think is appropriate at the time. Base your decisions on school policies and classroom rules and procedures. Here are a few things for you to consider:

- Stop the behavior immediately. If you overhear a student making a rude remark to a classmate, speak with the disruptive student privately. If the class hears the comments, you should address the situation with the class because the comments affect everyone, directly or indirectly.
- Give an "I message" to the disruptive student and **one warning**. Remain calm in the process. Remind the student of the rule associated with the disruptive behavior and the consequences, if he or she should make those or other rude remarks again. Sometimes, the disruptive student will respond by implicating the other student involved: "Well, he called me a name first. You didn't say anything to him." In this kind of situation, tell both students that you will speak with them privately after class to help them work through the problem. Attempt to get the two students to agree to this approach to resolving the issue. You may also want the school administrator who handles discipline problems at the after-class conference.
  If both students agree to the after-class meeting, and do not appear angry, redirect their attention to their class work. Give them a few seconds to make the transition. Then, move on with the other class activities. Monitor the two students' behaviors closely during the remainder of the period.

If one or both students in this situation do not agree to the meeting or appear upset by the incident, call the appropriate school administrator via class phone or intercom system to come to the room to meet with the two students privately.

Here are three things that I suggest you **avoid doing** in this or similar disruptive situations:

- Do not ask a disruptive student to stand in the hall until you can speak privately with him or her. The student could become involved in an altercation with another student while standing in the hall. Additionally, this student could leave the area or the school grounds.
- Do not send a disruptive student to the school office without first notifying the office *before* the student leaves the room. Otherwise, once the student leaves the room, he or she may decide to spend the remainder of the class period wandering the halls or hanging out in the bathroom.
- Do not have another student who is not involved in the problem escort the disruptive student to the school office. The disruptive student could become more irate about the situation and take out his or her frustration or anger on the other student.

Remember, you are responsible for every student "assigned to you" on any given school day and the decisions you make regarding each one.

Managing Aggressive Student Behavior

Aggressive behaviors include any student disruption that has the potential to become verbally or physically confrontational or hostile. These behaviors may be:

- Student to student
- Student to substitute teacher
- Class to substitute teacher

Usually, an aggressive act follows one or more precipitating acts. A substitute teacher who carefully monitors students' behavior during the class period and is attentive to various triggers that can cause disruptions can prevent some aggressive student behaviors from occurring. For example, two students are playfully hitting each other in class when, suddenly, one student hits the other student quite hard. In response, the student who received the harder than anticipated hit shoves the other student. A fight ensues between the two. The substitute teacher might have prevented this fight, if he or she had stopped the playful hitting as soon as the two students began.

Not all hostile student behavior in the classroom is a result of some precipitating factor that occurs in the classroom. Quite often, students bring to the classroom unresolved issues from other classes, the school bus, the hall, and the community. The problem escalates. Then, the students involved decide to "settle it" in your classroom.

In some situations, this same scenario can also be applicable when a student becomes confrontational with the substitute teacher. The substitute teacher becomes the "human target" of a student who is frustrated and angry over some unresolved issue that began someplace else. As a result, the student vents his negative feelings to the substitute.

With all aggressive or hostile student disruptions or situations that are highly likely to become confrontational, call for an appropriate school administrator to come to the room immediately. Do not try to handle the situation alone.

Classroom teachers and school administrators understand that substitute teachers cannot possibly prevent every student behavioral problem from occurring in the classroom, but they know that substitutes can greatly reduce the number of disruptive incidents if they (a) carefully monitor students' behavior and (b) immediately address the disruptions when they occur.

Conclusion

Substitute teaching is a very challenging profession. At times, you may feel like a juggler in the classroom as you try to attend to classroom management tasks, deal with student behavioral problems, and teach the teacher's lesson plan or the instructional activities that you create.

To make your substitute teaching experiences easier, more enjoyable, and productive, attend workshops that your school district offers to help you hone your skills. Talk to other substitute teachers, full-time teachers, and school administrators to share ideas and concerns, and seek answers to your questions. Thoroughly prepare for every substitute teaching experience. At the end of the day, reflect on the event to determine what pleases you most about the experience and what, if anything, you can do differently next time to improve.

One day, when you least expect, a student or former student will walk up to you and thank you for being a positive influence in his or her life. At that moment, you will understand how notable and rewarding it can be to substitute *teach*.

Appendix

You will always need information, materials, and supplies throughout your career to help you prepare and organize for your substitute teaching experiences. You should be able to find thousands of helpful tips and suggestions, easily, in several key places. To begin, visit the library media centers in the schools that you serve. You will probably find in the professional area for teachers, books, magazines, journals, CDs, and other materials filled with ideas and strategies. Also, visit your local libraries, bookstores, educational supplies centers, and stores that carry educational materials and supplies. Talk with teachers and school administrators. Many of these educators have personal copies of books and journals that they would be pleased to give you.

Also, browse the Worldwide Web. There is an enormous amount of information on the Internet and the good thing about all the information is that it is just a click away twenty-four hours a day, seven days a week. As you well know, websites move or close and information regarding services or products change. So be prepared to encounter a few inconveniences when you try to click on a site. Begin your search by visiting the websites listed on the next two pages. I hope you will find these sites helpful and easy to use.

Remember, too, that **Avenegg, Inc.**, has a long list of services and publications for your use. Featured on page 124 is our **Substitute Teacher Booster Bag**. On page 125, we feature our **IMaST** that we pack with over 40 different items. A **Quick Order Form** is available for your convenience on page 126. Most of the charts, checklists, planners, and exercises found in this book are available as single copies or as a complete packet from Avenegg, Inc. These publications are also available on a CD-ROM. Visit our Website for a complete list of the publications, products, gifts, discounts, and **FREE** materials that we offer. Our Website address is http://www.aveneggincpublishing.com

Also, please contact us if you should need additional materials or assistance to plan and organize your substitute teaching experiences. To school districts that are interested in designing and implementing a substitute teacher program, or providing your substitute teachers with professional development training, call us. We are here to serve. Here is how you can contact us:

Avenegg, Inc.

1147 S. Salisbury Blvd., Ste. 8
PMB 142
Salisbury, MD 21801
Tel: 1-410-572-8801
Toll Free: 1-888-572-8801
Fax: 1-410-742-7188
E-mail: info@aveneggincpublishing.com
Website Address: www.aveneggincpublishing.com

Website Resources for Substitute Teachers

Visit the following websites for sample lesson plans, themes, tips, crossword puzzle makers, printables, and more.

abcteach
http://abcteach.com

A to Z Teacher Stuff
http://www.atozteacherstuff.com/go/new.cgi

edHelper.com
http://www.edhelper.com

EduHound
http:// www.eduhound.com

Education Planet
http://www.lessonplanet.com

Education World
http://www.education-world.com

English.com
http://www.mes-english.com

Family Education Network
http://www.fen.com

Free Clipart Pictures.net
http://www.free-clipart-pictures.net

Freeology.com
http://freeology.com

Free Online Crossword Puzzle Maker
www.wigal.com/free-online-crossword-puzzle-maker

Gamequarium
http://gamequarium.com

Guest Teacher
http://www.guest-teacher.com

Houghton Mifflin
http://www.eduplace.com

Lesson Planning Center
http://www.teachervision.fen.com/teaching-methods/curriculum-planning/5775.html

Lesson Plans Page.com
http://www.lessonplanspage.com

Literature Lesson Plans
http://www.litplans.com

Middle School.Net
http://www.middleschool.net/MainFeatures/subteach

Mr. Peel's HistoryClassroom.com
www.HistoryClassroom.com

National Council of Teachers of Mathematics
http://www.nctm.org

National Education Association (NEA)
http://www.nea.org/tips/relate/subs.html

Preschool Lesson Plans
http://www.funlessonplans.com

SchoolExpress.com
http://www.schoolexpress.com

Songs for Teachers.com
http://www.songs4teachers.com

Substitute Teacher Resources
www.teachervision.fen.com

Teacher Planet
http://www.teacherplanet.com/calendar/05-SUM-06.htm

Teachers.Net
http://www.teachers.net/info/contacts.html

Teaching Tips
http://www.teachingtips.com/index.html

The Best on the Web for Teachers
http://teachers.teach-nology.com/index.html

The Biology Corner
http://www.biologycorner.com

The Teacher's Corner
http://www.theteacherscorner.net/privacypolicy.htm

Resources from Avenegg, Inc. for Substitute Teachers

Substitute Teacher Booster Bag

ORDER # ST203   Priced at $28.95

Every substitute needs a "confidence booster" at times. That is why we filled the **Substitute Teacher Booster Bag** with lots of great materials and supplies. Also included is a **white coffee mug, custom printed with "Happy Apple" and the words** *I Come to Teach!* We have packaged everything in a large, attractive *"Happy Apple," I Come to Teach!* tri-color, zipper tote bag, that a substitute can use again and again.

The **Substitute Teacher Booster Bag** is a terrific gift for every substitute. Here is what we have included in the zipper tote:

- 1 12-oz "Happy Apple," *I Come to Teach!* white, coffee mug
- 1 Apple key tag. The front of the tag reads "Behind every successful school is a team"; the back of the tag reads "A + substitute teachers."
- 1 35 x 5/8 lanyard, with a breakaway and a removable end buckle; custom printed on the lanyard are the words "A+ Substitute Teacher."
- Over 100 assorted motivational stickers
- 35 positive reinforcement certificates
- 1 copy of *I Come to Teach!* This 128-page paperback is a comprehensive guide and planner for substitute teachers. The book is filled with tips, strategies, activities, checklists, planners, and more.
- 5 copies of *The Substitute Teacher Planning Log.* With this 4-page planning log, substitutes will never have to walk into the classroom unprepared again.
- 5 copies of *The Substitute Teacher Organizer.* How can substitutes organize for their substitute teaching experiences and stay organized during the day? How can they possibly remember all of the things they need to do? This 18-page reminder breaks it all down into six areas, with a checklist of things "to do" in each area.
- 5 copies of *The Substitute Teacher End of the Day Summary for the Regular Teacher.* No longer does a substitute need to scribble several notes about his or her day to the teacher; the sub can leave a brief, concise, four-page report that every classroom teacher, who has a substitute, will greatly appreciate.
- 5 copies of *The Substitute Teacher End of the Day Summary for the Principal.* This two-page summary is a great tool for a substitute to use to share his or her thoughts with the principal about the substitute teaching experience. The completed summary helps to keep the principal informed of the various successes and challenges that substitutes are experiencing in the school.

To place your order, use the Quick Order Form on page 126 or visit our Website at http://www.aveneggincpublishing.com.

Instructional Materials and Supplies Tote (IMaST)

Order # ST204 $39.95   "OVER 40 Different ITEMS"

- **Never walk into the classroom unprepared again.**
- **Prepare for those situations when you may not have the teacher's lesson plan.**

We can help! First, we will give you a large attractive "I Come to Teach!" super-size tote bag. This bag is your *Instructional Materials and Supplies Tote* (IMaST). Then, we will pack your bag with general supplies, age-appropriate books, learning activities and other items that will help you have an exceptionally good substitute teaching experience. Your bag will be packed and ready to go whenever you are called to substitute. Here are a few "tools of the trade" that you will receive in your tote.

- ❑ I Come to Teach! coffee mug
- ❑ A+ substitute teacher lanyard
- ❑ The Substitute Teacher Planning Log (10 copies)
- ❑ The Substitute Teacher Organizer (10 copies)
- ❑ Large picture books (Pre-K through elementary)
- ❑ High-interest materials for middle and high school students
- ❑ Filler-activities
- ❑ Flashcards
- ❑ Brain games
- ❑ Stuffed animals
- ❑ Children songs (CD)
- ❑ Pencils
- ❑ Erasers
- ❑ Ballpoint pens (red, black, and blue)
- ❑ Highlighters (a variety of colors)
- ❑ Transparency markers
- ❑ Magic markers
- ❑ Crayons
- ❑ Rulers
- ❑ Paper clips
- ❑ Ministapler
- ❑ Staples
- ❑ Scissors
- ❑ Tape (Scotch tape and masking tape)
- ❑ 3x5 note cards
- ❑ 5x8 note cards
- ❑ Post-its
- ❑ Stickers
- ❑ Motivational certificates
- ❑ Chalk
- ❑ Board eraser

- ❑ Blank transparencies
- ❑ Notebook paper
- ❑ Pocket portfolios
- ❑ Construction paper
- ❑ Timer
- ❑ Nametags
- ❑ Help tents
- ❑ Rubber ball
- ❑ Tissues
- ❑ Instant antiseptic hand cleanser

AND MORE!!!

I Come to Teach!

Avenegg, Inc.

TWO EASY WAYS TO ORDER

1. ONLINE:

http://www.aveneggincpublishing.com

<table>
<tr><td>Customer Identification Number

Priority Code: ST1006
Preferred Customer: YES</td></tr>
</table>

2. MAIL ORDER FORM TO:

Avenegg, Inc.
1147 S. Salisbury Blvd. Ste. 8
PMB 142
Salisbury, MD 21801

NAME _____

STREET ADDRESS _____

CITY _____ STATE _____ ZIP _____

PHONE: DAY ( )_____ EVE ( ) _____

EMAIL _____

Method of Payment

***CREDIT CARDS ARE ACCEPTED ONLY WITH ONLINE ORDERS.
***CHECKS AND MONEY ORDERS ARE ACCEPTED WITH MAIL ORDERS.

Enclosed with Order Form
- ❑ **Check**
- ❑ **Money Order**

Get an additional $10 off this order - if you spend $75 or more!!!

ITEM #	QTY.	PRICE	DESCRIPTION/TITLE	AMOUNT

Mail Orders
Shipping & Handling
USA and Canada

$0-$15.00, add $5
$15.01-$25, add $6
$25.01-$50, add $7
$50.01-$100, add $8
$100+ will be charged actual shipping charges. Add $10 plus regular shipping charges for UPS 2nd day air.

Subtotal	
Additional Savings: **Spend $75 or more - Save $10**	
MD residents: Add 5% tax	
Shipping	
Total	

- ❑ Please send a **FREE Newsletter** to my friend.
- ❑ Please send a **discount coupon** to my friend.

Name _____
Address _____
City _____ State _____ Zip _____
Email _____

126

Index